BILL:
An American Doctor in China

By
Ann Lovell

Based on the book, *Bill Wallace of China*
By Jesse Fletcher

Proceeds from the sale of this book will benefit
IMB's Lottie Moon Christmas Offering®
for International Missions

Cover art by Mike Mirabella

You Can Share Good News

When I was four years old, two men from our town knocked on our door and invited my family to come to church. We went and I learned about Jesus. Four years later, when I was eight years old, my pastor visited our home to talk to one of my brothers about the gospel and what it would mean for him to put his trust in Jesus and follow Jesus as Lord. Both of my brothers and I were saved that day. Looking back, I realize that the people who came to our house were just regular people but people who were on mission with God, telling others about Jesus.

In many parts of the world, there are no churches or Christians to tell the good news about Jesus. That's why God calls regular people to leave their home and their country, travel to distant lands, and share the good news. These people are missionaries. They are regular people who are on mission with God and their mission field is overseas. They have the most important job in all the world! Without them, entire countries of people will miss out on the good news about Jesus.

Many missionaries travel to dangerous places and make huge sacrifices in order to answer God's call and share the good news with those who haven't heard. Bill Wallace was one of those missionaries. As you learn about him, ask God to show you where He wants you to share the good news about Jesus. Whether it's at home or overseas, God wants all of us to be on mission with Him!

Paul Chitwood
President, International Mission Board
Jan. 2019

Contents

Chapter 1: Who Was Bill Wallace?

Bill Wallace stood on the dock of Guangzhou in southern China. His meeting with other missionaries was finished. He was ready to sail home to Wuzhou, China. He had work to do.

It was 1938. Bill was a missionary doctor at the Stout Memorial Hospital. The Imperial Japanese Army was taking over China. The Japanese had attacked the hospital two times before.

At the docks no boats were sailing. Boat captains had canceled their trips. Bill stood on the dock trying to decide what to do next. Suddenly air raid sirens tore through the morning. Hundreds of people scrambled for safety. Bill watched as Japanese planes flew into the harbor. The planes fired red tracer bullets that cut into boat after boat. Then Bill realized the guns were firing at him! He ran for shelter behind some freight boxes. A few seconds later machine gun fire splintered the dock where he had been standing!

Now, Bill decided he did not need to get home so badly! Instead he ran low and fast to the home of Gene and Louise Hill. Bill had stayed with the Hills during the meeting.

When Gene and Louise came in, they found Bill lying across a bed. Propping up on one elbow, Bill grinned and said, "You know, a guy could killed out there!"

Bill had been in China two years. This brush with war was one of his first in China. It wouldn't be his last.

Chapter 2: Bill Finds God's Purpose

Bill Wallace was born January 19, 1908, in Knoxville, Tennessee. His father was a doctor, and the family was active at Broadway Baptist Church. Bill enjoyed being part of the Royal Ambassadors, a mission organization for boys, at his church.

Bill's mother died when he was 11. His father and grandmother raised him and his sister, Ruth. Bill became shy after his mother died, and he was very close to his father.

As a boy, Bill loved cars. He was an average student and a talented mechanic. Many people thought he might grow up to become a mechanic. God had other plans.

One summer day when Bill was 17 years old, he was working on a car in his garage. His small New Testament was open on the workbench beside his tools. A thought came to his mind. He slowed from his work, and then started working again. The thought came again, more strongly, and caused him to make a mistake. The third time the thought came,

Bill stopped what he was doing and picked up his New Testament. Maybe, he thought, the Bible could give him some answer for the question his mind was asking.

The thought that kept coming to his mind was this: What should I do with my life? Or better: What does God want me to do with my life?

Looking through his New Testament, Bill believed God was calling him to be a medical missionary. Before now, he had never considered being a doctor or a missionary. He was going to trade school to be a mechanic. But when God spoke to Bill's heart, Bill said, "Yes!"

Bill wrote God's purpose for his life in his New Testament. Later he handed the New Testament to his sister, Ruth Lynn. He told her what he had decided. The date was July 5, 1925.

Chapter 3: A Hospital Needs a Surgeon

The Stout Memorial Hospital in Wuzhou, China, had been treating patients since 1904. Dr. Robert Beddoe was working in a small office in the hospital. The office was hot. Wiping the sweat from his neck, the doctor paused from his typing. He looked out the small window. How could he explain what he needed to his boss in America? He started typing.

```
We have a long history at
Stout Memorial Hospital.
Southern Baptists can
be proud of what has
been done in the name of
the Lord Jesus Christ.
However, without a
surgeon the hospital will
not be able to help the
people.
```

```
We must have another
missionary doctor, a
surgeon who can come in
and do things I have not
been able to do. … I
repeat. We must have a
surgeon.
```

Dr. Beddoe folded the letter and stuffed it in the envelope. He looked out the window to see a long line of patients waiting to get into the clinic.

"O God, give us a surgeon," he prayed.

Chapter 4: Bill Writes a Letter

Bill was working the night shift at Knoxville General Hospital. He was the chief surgical resident. He had just finished writing a letter to the Foreign Mission Board (now the International Mission Board) of the Southern Baptist Convention in Richmond, Virginia. Before he folded it, he read it one more time:

My name is William L. Wallace. I am now serving as a resident in surgery at Knoxville General Hospital, Knoxville, Tennessee.

Since my senior year in high school, I felt God wanted me to be a medical missionary. I have been preparing myself since then. I attended the University of Tennessee and received the M.D. from the

University Medical School in
Memphis. I did an internship
here at Knoxville General
and remained for a surgical
residency.

I am not sure what
information you need. I am
single, twenty-six years old,
and a member of the Broadway
Baptist Church. My mother
died when I was eleven. My
father, also a physician,
passed away two years ago.
There were only two of us,
and my sister, Ruth Lynn, is
planning marriage.

I must confess I am not
a good speaker or teacher.
I do feel God can use my
training as a physician. As
humbly as I know how, I
want to volunteer to serve
as a medical missionary under
our Southern Baptist Foreign
Mission Board.

I have always thought
of Africa, but I will go
anywhere I am needed.

Bill folded the letter. He placed it in an
envelope addressed to the Foreign Mission
Board. He got up from the night nurse's desk

and walked down the hall to the mail drop. Outside, the sun was just beginning to rise.

Chapter 5: Two Letters

Dr. Charles Maddry was president of the Foreign Mission Board in 1934. Things had been tough for the mission organization. Dr. Maddry hoped that was about to change. Then, he received two letters: one from Dr. Beddoe in China and one from Dr. Wallace in Knoxville, Tennessee. The letter from China spelled out the need. The Stout Memorial Hospital needed a surgeon. The letter from Knoxville answered the need. Bill Wallace wanted to volunteer as a surgeon, wherever God led him.

Was this coincidence? Dr. Maddry didn't think so. God worked this way. Here was proof that God's purposes are greater than any challenge he might face.

Dr. Maddry thought to himself, Dr. Wallace, meet Dr. Beddoe. You are the answer to his prayers, only you don't know it yet.

Before he could introduce Dr. Beddoe to Dr. Wallace, Dr. Maddry had to do some checking on Bill. He could not send Bill all the way around the world to China if he was not trained and ready. He also needed to make sure Bill was a man of Christian character. Dr. Maddry sent some letters of his own to check on the young surgeon. All the letters he received in response were positive. Dr. Maddry decided it was time to meet Bill Wallace in person.

Dr. Maddry arranged to meet Bill in November 1934 in Knoxville. Dr. Maddry was pleased with the young man. Bill was likable. He was also excited about being a missionary. Dr. Maddry wrote Dr. Beddoe:

> I now have hopes for you in the person of a fine young man, William L. Wallace, General Hospital, Knoxville, Tennessee. He is thoroughly prepared and from all I can gather, is a splendid young man. ... I think he is going to be the man.

Still, Bill had to make one more decision.

Chapter 6: What Will Bill Do?

Dr. Dewey Peters and Bill's father had been good friends. Dr. Peters called Bill one day shortly after his interview with Dr. Maddry. He asked Bill to come by his office. Dr. Peters had been Bill's Sunday School teacher. Bill wanted to talk with Dr. Peters about being a missionary. As the two men talked, Dr. Peters offered Bill some advice: "Make up your mind now to practice only the best medicine throughout all your life."

Bill nodded. It was good advice, and he would never forget it.

But Dr. Peters had another idea he wanted to discuss with Bill.

"I've been giving it a lot of thought, and I feel good about it," Dr. Peters said. "I would like for you to come in with me and share my practice. ... In time, it can become a full partnership."

Dr. Peters did not have to tell Bill that the job would pay very well. The offer was a big temptation. It was any young doctor's dream. It was also a test of Bill's understanding of God's leadership.

Bill thanked Dr. Peters. For several days, he prayed. He knew the money was good, but money did not interest him. Fame also wasn't important to him. So why was Bill tempted by Dr. Peters' offer? Bill was tempted because this job would give him the opportunity to perfect his skills as a doctor. He wasn't sure he would be able to learn new things as a missionary in China.

But after days of prayer, Bill realized he could not abandon the call of God. God had called him and trained him for a different type of life. He knew his destiny was to serve the people of China. He went back to see Dr. Peters. He thanked him for his offer, but he explained that God had called him to be a missionary. Dr. Peters understood. As Bill left Dr. Peters' office, Bill felt a deep sense of peace. He remembered a letter Dr. Beddoe had sent him from China.

```
I have asked Dr. Maddry
for a surgeon. It appears
that you may be the man
for this job. I hope and
pray that this may be
true. … If you are the
man, I pray you may come
quickly. The time is
short. … I hope you are
that man.
```

Bill silently prayed that he was that man.

1934 turned to 1935. Bill filled out lots of forms for the Foreign Mission Board. In May, he received another letter. If he could be in Richmond in July, the leaders at the Foreign Mission Board would talk with him. If he passed the test, he could sail for China no later than September.

Bill traveled to Richmond in late July. On July 24, 1935, the leaders of the Board met with him. They asked him a lot of questions about his school, God's call, and his commitment to missions. They decided Bill was ready for the work God had called him to do in China.

On July 25, 1935, the Foreign Mission Board appointed Bill Wallace to be a medical missionary to Wuzhou, China. It had been ten years since God first called him to be a medical missionary.

Chapter 7: Bill Sails for China

Bill sailed for China from San Francisco harbor on September 6, 1935. The Sunday before had been "Bill Wallace Day" at Broadway Baptist Church in Knoxville. The people in Bill's church gave an offering that Sunday that was enough to pay his first year's salary and many other expenses. The Foreign Mission Board would have paid those costs, but the people at Broadway wanted to help. It was their job to help him, they said.

After the sermon, the pastor asked Bill to speak to the church. Bill did not like speaking in front of large groups.

"I really don't know what to say," Bill said. "I guess it's a good thing I'm a doctor."

The people laughed.

"Maybe I ought to say this, though. Many people have asked me why I do not stay, with all the work there is to be done right here. I am not sure I know just what I should say to them, but I do know I'm going to China because God is leading me there."

After church, nearly two hundred people went with Bill to the train station. This was hard for Bill, not only because he was leaving his friends and family, but also because he did not like the attention.

Now, a week later, he was on a steamship to China. He loved the memories, but he knew it was time to look forward. He did not know what was ahead. There would be no turning back.

Chapter 8: Bill's First Glimpse of China

In October 1935, Bill's steamship sailed into Hong Kong harbor. Many different sounds, sights and smells greeted him. As Bill leaned over the rail, an older missionary came to stand beside him.

"You are joining quite a heritage," the older man said. "Missionaries have been here since the eighth century. But in 1724, the Manchus made Christianity illegal. They almost destroyed the work here."

Bill listened as the man continued talking. The man said many early missionaries only lived a few years after arriving in China. He talked about the Boxer Rebellion of 1900, when the government killed hundreds of missionaries and Chinese Christians. Now, though, in 1935 people thought Christians were safe in China. They hoped men and women would never again have to die for their faith. Neither Bill nor the older missionary knew what was ahead.

Bill enjoyed talking with the missionary, but soon the boat docked. It was time to start his new life in China!

When Bill stepped off the boat, Dr. Beddoe was there to meet him. This day was an answer to Dr. Beddoe's prayers. He was so excited!

The next day, Bill and Dr. Beddoe boarded another boat to Wuzhou. It took two more days to get there. Bill enjoyed seeing the sights of the countryside. Soon, Bill saw the buildings of Wuzhou and then the hospital. He had pictured it many times. Now, he was finally here.

When the boat arrived at the dock, the missionaries and hospital staff greeted him. As the group walked through the streets to the hospital, Bill heard pigs squeal and smelled fish and meat for sale in the market. He stepped past rickshaws and bicycles. There was too much to see! Then he stood at the entrance to Stout Memorial Hospital.

The building was five stories tall. There was also a two-story clinic and a few small homes. A wall surrounded the buildings and a sloping yard. At the entrance to the hospital, the entire hospital staff stood to greet the new doctor. Everyone was happy to see him!

It was evening before Bill could be alone again. He walked through the gardens inside the hospital compound and looked across the city of Wuzhou to the West River. The sun was setting. A cool breeze was blowing. Bill thanked God for the opportunity before him.

By the fourth day in Wuzhou, Bill

performed emergency surgery. He impressed the nurses and interns with his skill and technique. The missionaries liked him, too. Bill was off to a good start.

After two weeks, Bill moved to Guangzhou to learn the Chinese language.

Dr. Beddoe wrote to Dr. Maddry:

```
Wallace has made a good
impression on the Chinese
people, which is the
most important thing a
new missionary can do.
Our workers have fallen
for him completely. His
wholesome smile and
evident interest in them
have won him to them
completely.
```

Chapter 9: Bill Learns Cantonese

Bill was ready for his first day of language school in Guangzhou. He was so excited he got to school early. He sat down in one of the two chairs in his classroom. Soon, Mr. Wong arrived. Mr. Wong was Bill's language teacher. Bill stood up when Mr. Wong entered the room.

Speaking in Cantonese, Mr. Wong said, "Sit down." He reached up to Bill's shoulder to push him back into his chair. Then, he smiled and said, again in Cantonese, "Get up." Mr. Wong lifted Bill back to his feet. Bill began to get the idea. Not a word of English was spoken.

Bill's language classes included mornings with Mr. Wong, private homework and then an afternoon class with a group of other new missionaries. The class included Gene and Louise Hill.

Cantonese is a hard language for an American to learn. It is a tonal language. That means the same sound can have different meanings depending on how it is used. Since Bill wasn't very musical, he had a hard time hearing the tones. Bill's friends in his class often laughed at the way he tried to say some of the words. But Bill took it well. He laughed with them.

Gene Hill became one of Bill's best friends. The two men spent a lot of time exploring Guangzhou and practicing their new language. The shopkeepers in Guangzhou enjoyed seeing Bill and Gene together and talking with them.

Bill's first Christmas away from Tennessee wasn't easy. He received a package from his sister with a photo of his mom and dad. Both his parents had been dead for several years. Their photo reminded him of happy memories from his childhood. Friends of his sister also wanted to send him something he could really use. Bill thought about it. He decided to ask them to subscribe to *Time* magazine or a medical journal called *Surgical Clinics of North America*.

Bill also went back to Wuzhou for two weeks during Christmas. At the hospital, he immediately went to work. He wrote his sister a short letter:

```
I went to Wuzhou and just
got back yesterday. I had
a good time. I operated.
```

Bill returned to Guangzhou and kept studying the language. He made many friends during that year of language study. Many of them were Chinese. Bill was learning the secret of being a good missionary: Loving the people.

Bill finished his first year in China with a trip to Hong Kong. He attended the annual South China Baptist Mission meeting in August 1936. After the mission meeting, Bill moved to Wuzhou. He was ready to get to work!

Chapter 10: Bill Gets to Work

When Bill got to Wuzhou, he found he was the only missionary there. War was beginning to brew between two different factions in China. Warlords lived in the province where Wuzhou was located. They were fighting with the national government headed by Chiang Kai-Shek. The other missionaries decided to wait out the crisis in Hong Kong. Bill got right to work. He performed surgery the day after he arrived.

That afternoon, an American naval officer from the ship, the *U.S.S. Mindanao*, came to the hospital. The captain of the ship offered to take Bill on board and take him back to Hong Kong, where he would be safe.

"Back to Hong Kong?" Bill said. "Why, I just got here! I'm not going anywhere, war or no war!"

"Begging your pardon, sir," the young man replied. "The captain feels he cannot be responsible for your safety if you stay in the city, even overnight."

Bill laughed. "Tell your captain to rest easy. He was not responsible for my coming here in the first place, and he doesn't need to be responsible for my staying here." Bill added more seriously, "But please tell him I appreciate his concern. I know he wanted to help. I just don't think I need it."

The young sailor left, and Bill got back to work. A few hours later, the sailor appeared again. The captain wanted to invite Bill to dinner on the ship.

"Your captain would not be trying to trick me into safety?" Bill asked, with a grin.

"No, sir. Today is his birthday, and he wanted another American to share it with him."

Bill was happy to accept. When he arrived, he found two other men were also at the party. They were oil company executives who were spending the next couple of days on board.

As the men got to know one another, the captain asked Bill, "Why would an able young surgeon like you give his life to a God-forsaken place like this?"

Bill smiled. He had heard the question before. "It's not an easy thing to explain," he said. "I am not running away from anything. I didn't leave a girlfriend behind, and the police aren't after me."

The men laughed, but the captain asked again, "But what makes a man feel he should do something like this?"

Bill said, "Well, my father was a doctor, but that was the last thing I wanted to be. My love was mechanics. A gasoline motor or even an electrical motor is still one of the most intriguing things in the world to me. But as a teenager, I came to experience a deep sense of unrest about what I was to do with my life. One day, I became very deeply convinced that I should become a medical missionary."

"Had you ever considered anything like that before?" One of the oilmen asked.

"No, I am certain no one had ever suggested it. My father was all set to help me get into the automobile business, but after that day, I was convinced this was what I should do."

Bill paused. Then he said, "That was eleven years ago now, and I have become more and more sure with each passing year that God was in this decision."

Looking through the porthole of the ship toward the hospital, he said, "I am convinced that happiness, fulfillment, and meaning for me lie right up there on that hill."

There was a long silence, and Bill was a little embarrassed. Soon the conversation went in other directions, but the men didn't forget the smiling young doctor from Tennessee.

Chapter 11: Bill Makes Sick People Well

The threat of war soon went away, and the missionaries returned to Wuzhou. Work at Stout Memorial Hospital began again. Bill operated every morning. He spent his afternoons studying language and his nights seeing the many patients who visited the hospital and clinic. Long before daylight, he would report to the hospital to study his cases and instruct his assistants. Before breakfast, he had usually completed an operation, or, if they were minor, several of them. He worked very long hours. The Chinese people gave him a Chinese name, Waa I Saang.

Bill was soon thanking God for the two years of surgery he had as a resident at Knoxville General. He wished he had three more. In a few weeks he performed operations he never expected to do. He met situations he wasn't sure how to handle. He removed large tumors and performed delicate eye operations. He began to acquire a reputation as a very good doctor.

Bill performed an operation on a little girl with a bad harelip. After the surgery, the child could talk clearly. Other children no longer teased the little girl. Her mother was so grateful! She went to see every sick person she knew and told them about the wonderful Waa I Saang in Wuzhou.

One day the mother heard of a woman who was upset because her son had a clubfoot. The husband had threatened to throw the child away. The grateful mother took her little girl and went to see the woman.

"Go to see Waa I Saang in Wuzhou!" the mother said. "See what he did to my child. She can talk clearly now and looks like other children, too. Waa I Saang can do anything. He can even give your child a new foot."

The story made Bill happy. He was glad that a child no longer had to be the butt of teasing and cruel jokes. Other times, though, Bill was sad and frustrated when he couldn't save the lives of sick people.

In one case, parents brought in their small child who had a very serious infection. Bill tried every possible kind of emergency treatment. Despite his efforts, the child died. Slowly Bill straightened his shoulders and sighed. Then he reached down and picked up the lifeless child. Gently holding the child in his arms, Bill sat down on the bed, looking into the closed eyes and still face. As the parents came into the room, Bill told them what had happened. His Cantonese was less-than-perfect, but his kindness was evident. Then he told them about Jesus and how much He loves little children.

Chapter 12: Sick People Hear About Jesus

More and more people came to the hospital as they heard the stories of sick people made well. Dr. Beddoe was so excited. Sick people were getting well, and they were hearing about Jesus! That fall he wrote Dr. Maddry in Richmond:

> The Board made no mistake selecting Dr. Wallace for this place. He has a sharp eye, a steady hand, and a good knowledge of surgery. I am sure he will build a reputation that will bring patients here even from Guangzhou.
>
> Best of all are the spiritual results. We had two cases of entire families deciding to

```
follow Jesus. Dr. Leung
joined our church
recently, and one of our
fine doctors, Miss Wang,
will be baptized Sunday.
Truly God has richly
blessed us this year.
```

These two Chinese doctors had taken great risks by choosing to follow Jesus against the traditions of their ancestors. Their lives reflected the power of Bill's witness among them. The Chinese had heard sermons before, but in Bill Wallace, they saw a person who loved Jesus and loved them. That made the difference.

Bill was very happy. He was needed, he was seeing people get well, and he was where he felt God wanted him.

Bill's second Christmas in China passed more easily than the first one. A little bit of Tennessee arrived with a big box of homemade fruitcake from Bill's sister and her husband. The mission staff exchanged small gifts, and Bill made a brief trip to Hong Kong for the holidays. Bill was happy. He felt like he belonged.

The situation in China seemed stable, but 1937 would bring hard times.

Chapter 13: War with Japan Begins

For five years the Japanese had been planning to take over China. After gaining control of Manchuria, they began taking over Chinese territory north of the Great Wall. This happened while the Chinese were fighting among themselves. Later, the Chinese groups came together to try to defeat the Japanese. Japan knew a united China would totally change a situation that had been going their way. Japan needed to move quickly if it wanted to take over China.

On the night of July 7, 1937, Japanese troops were practicing field maneuvers across the river from China's capital of Beijing. At the Marco Polo Bridge, someone fired a shot. The Japanese quickly claimed they had been assaulted and launched a massive "retaliation." War had begun.

The days and weeks that followed shocked the world. The Japanese crushed the Chinese wherever they met them. They killed millions of men, women, and children.

Bill Wallace and the missionaries at Stout Memorial Hospital were following these events closely. The North China Mission was immediately involved. The stories that came back from missionaries in North China were not pretty. Many missionaries decided to stay through the Japanese assault. They hoped to carry on their work as best they could behind the lines. Also, Bill and his friends knew the West River Basin from Guangzhou to Nanking would be a prime target for the Japanese. Stout Memorial Hospital was right in the middle.

Chapter 14: Missionaries Choose

As the war continued, the situation in Wuzhou grew worse. Thousands of Chinese troops went to Guangzhou and then north to fight the Japanese. Soon the people heard reports that many had been killed. The people were sad and scared. Then the Japanese bombed Guangzhou and the railroad. Finally, they blockaded the river.

The river was the only means that the team at Stout Memorial Hospital could get supplies. Now the doctors were faced with shortages of food and medical supplies. Fortunately, Dr. Beddoe was a wise man. He was able to find supplies when the hospital needed them most. As it turned out, he had stored many needed items before the war that the doctors were able to use when they could not get supplies from outside.

Dr. Beddoe was also concerned for the Baptist hospital at Guilin, a Baptist mission station farther west and north in the

Guangxi Province. That hospital needed an administrator. Soon it would have to close. Dr. Beddoe wanted to go there and save the institution. But he decided not to go. He was afraid Bill wasn't ready to take over the hospital.

Dr. Beddoe felt this way for several good reasons. First, Bill only wanted to be a doctor. He had no interest in running the hospital. He referred everything about running the hospital to Dr. Beddoe, even when people asked for his opinion. Also, Bill seemed to be a soft touch for the Chinese. He did not like to charge money for his services, and the Chinese people knew that. Finally, as a manager, Bill let both nurses and doctors choose their own pace. He was never heard to scold any of them. Dr. Beddoe saw these behaviors as weaknesses.

But there was another side to the story. Bill wanted to avoid any sign that he might want Dr. Beddoe's job. He also loved to focus only on medicine and his patients. He liked leaving the details to Dr. Beddoe. While it was true he led the hospital staff quietly, they still followed him enthusiastically. They would do whatever Dr. Wallace asked. It was also true that he didn't completely understand Chinese culture, but his lack of understanding was balanced by his love for the Chinese people.

In late October, Dr. Beddoe no longer had time to think about these issues. The American consul had warned the hospital staff to prepare to evacuate. The mission group was forced to talk about what they would do in case the order came. Japanese planes had not yet been seen over Wuzhou skies, but the missionaries knew they were probably on the way soon. When the planes came, the missionaries knew the bombs would also bring lots of destruction and suffering. The staff, and especially the missionaries, realized they had strong ties to the hospital.

The hospital had an unbroken ministry since 1904. The missionaries did not want the hospital's ministry to end, even if the Japanese took over. After their first meeting, they wrote Dr. Maddry:

```
We at the hospital have
decided to stay under
all conditions. We feel
that now is the time when
every hospital in China
should be open.
```

Chapter 15: Air Raid

On December 19, 1937, Bill Wallace opened his eyes. He lay still until he could see in the darkness. The only light was a faint shaft coming from the hospital across the garden. He quietly slipped out of bed. He had lived in a room in Dr. Beddoe's house since coming to Wuzhou. He did not want to wake the family. He dressed and slipped outside.

Within moments he was visiting wards, checking patients, and reading the night nurse's reports. After checking on some patients, he returned to his small office to study X-rays. He made a few notes, then yawned and stretched. Bill was content and happy serving God in Wuzhou.

Thumbing the pages of his New Testament—the same one in which he had marked his determination to be a medical missionary—he began his morning devotions. He read a brief passage of Scripture, gave some thought to it, and bowed his head for a brief prayer. His devotions rarely lasted very long. In a few moments he walked out on the porch of the hospital to greet the dawn.

Bill liked the way dawn came at Wuzhou. He liked how the sunrise highlighted the river, the mist, the boats, and the nets. Smiling and very happy, he took the steps three at a time and jogged toward the Beddoe house to have breakfast with Dr. and Mrs. Beddoe and Rex Ray.

"Howdy, Bill," said the friendly Texan, Rex Ray. "I was just explaining to Dr. Beddoe my plan for running the Japanese blockade next spring to get the medical supplies you are going to need."

"I am afraid our cowboy adventurer is anxious to relive the old days," Dr. Beddoe said. A Chinese bandit had captured Rex Ray ten years before. Rex loved telling about the exciting adventure. "But I hardly think the plan is wise, despite the fact we will have some very critical needs by spring."

"What's your plan, Parson?" Bill liked to talk with the determined old missionary, whom he had nicknamed, Parson, which means "pastor."

Enthusiastically, Rex began to outline his plan. "You see, I have this friend who owns a boat in Guangzhou ..."

Dr. Beddoe interrupted him. "If you ask me, Guangzhou won't be in Chinese hands by spring. They bombed it again this morning, and eighteen Japanese warships are reported on their way to begin a bombardment."

"That doesn't sound good," Bill said. He

had meant to get back in time that morning to listen to the news with Dr. Beddoe, but he wasn't able to.

Suddenly an air raid siren broke the morning peace. The three men had heard it before in practice drills, but this was the real thing. They could hear for themselves the distant roar of planes. They ran down the steps from the house and across to the hospital.

Many people were scared. Working calmly, Bill, Rex and Dr. Beddoe organized the excited staff and quieted the terrified patients. Then, beginning with the top floor, they moved the more serious patients to the basement. By this time they could hear bombs exploding and the chatter of machine guns. The patients who could walked down the steps, helping those who could not. If the bombs hit the hospital, they would have to go through five floors of concrete. While the builders could not have foreseen the need, they had built an excellent bomb shelter.

As soon as the patients were safely in the basement, Bill bounded up the five flights of stairs to the roof to watch the sky. There were eleven planes in flight. A big red rising sun emblem sparkled from the nearest. These were Japanese planes!

The first bombs fell nearly a mile away at Wuzhou's airport. The bombs completely demolished the hangar with the Chinese planes. Then the pilots tried to destroy an electrical plant. Failing, they circled for a second pass. Again they missed, but this time the bombs fell nearer the hospital, and the explosion shook the building, shattering glass.

It was over as quickly as it began. As the planes disappeared over the hill back of the hospital, the "all clear" sounded. Bill looked over the city. Fires blazed in more than a dozen places, and smoke covered the city. People were running everywhere. Bill later explained that he would never be the same again. The attacks might get worse, much worse, but there was nothing like the first time!

Chapter 16: Trial by Fire

Dr. Beddoe was firm. "I think we ought to go ahead and talk about it now," he said.

The Wuzhou missionaries were gathered for an informal meeting in the Beddoes' living room. Dr. Beddoe feared the Japanese would eventually attack South China, beginning with Guangzhou.

"If Guangzhou falls, they may move right up the river to Wuzhou."

Rex Ray spoke, "You can bet your bottom dollar, if they start in here to take us, they will try to level us to the ground with their bombers first. I am not sure there would be enough of us left to worry about when they got here."

"I don't agree," Dr. Beddoe said. "Air raids will not close this hospital. We can take a direct hit or even several hits on our roof and still stand. I know this building; I built it."

"Well, they may be unable to level the building," Bill said. Standing at the window, he was looking up at the gray stone structure. "I agree with you there. But it's kind of difficult to carry on much of a hospital if all the equipment, windows, and doors are shattered. Maybe we ought to set up emergency operating facilities in the basement where the bombs are least likely to do serious damage."

He had thought about this a lot. He was glad for the opportunity to introduce the idea.

"I think Bill's right," Mrs. Beddoe said. "It won't be too difficult to set it up if we start now."

Dr. Beddoe nodded. "I agree, but the thing I'm trying to point out is that military occupation is another matter altogether."

They had all heard stories of how badly the Japanese troops treated civilians, especially women and children.

"I am unwilling to ask these nurses to remain at their posts and run the risk of attack by drunken soldiers," Dr. Beddoe said.

The group nodded silently.

Surprisingly, Bill, who seldom offered advice, spoke again. "Let's protect ourselves against air raids now and concern ourselves with invasion when it comes. I doubt we can make much advance preparation in that direction anyhow."

A murmur of approval came from the others. It was not a note of resignation, but one of "Let's work while it's day; we know the night is coming." Bill believed strongly in the Scripture passage which, in effect, says, "As your days are, so shall your strength be."

Two months later the bombers returned.

This time it was a much larger squadron of planes. Following the bomb run, they turned and came in low, machine gunning all who could not find cover.

Though the missionaries had finished building the emergency operating room, the attack caught Bill in regular surgery. He barely had time to finish and move his patient to a safe place in a hallway away from flying glass when the first bombs fell. Again the hospital was spared, though much glass was broken by concussion from the bombs. The number of wounded brought in following the raid was twice that of the first raid.

Efforts to repair the damage done by the bombs continued far into the night. Bill was doing a totally different kind of surgery now. He was trying to put together those badly mangled by the bombs. The work was hard and difficult.

Weeks later, tired and exasperated, Bill said to a Chinese colleague, "I sometimes feel like I am plowing in the sea."

"You should take a vacation," his colleague replied.

Chapter 17: Bill Takes a Vacation

Missionaries serving with the Foreign Mission Board were supposed to take a month each year for rest and renewal. Bill had taken only one week in three years. With the Japanese overrunning much of China, he decided he should see some of the country now. He would visit the interior of China. He would live like the Chinese for a while. After all, Dr. Beddoe was always saying Bill did not understand the Chinese. Bill decided the vacation would give him some time to work through the depression and frustration settling over him.

Dr. Beddoe had strong reservations about Bill's vacation. Bill wanted to go west to Chongqing and Chengdu. He would leave Cantonese-speaking territory and would be unable to communicate. Bill said he still could read it, and he could always contact missionaries in the area. Seeing that his colleague had his mind made up, Dr. Beddoe agreed to let him go.

The last week in March 1938, Bill performed an incredible number of surgeries so he could leave without any known need unmet. Then, exhausted, he left by bus on the first day of April.

His first day of travel was over low mountains. The bus was crowded and hot. It was filled with a babble of voices and strange smells. Despite the discomfort, Bill found himself relaxing. He enjoyed the countryside with its dazzling green blanket of new rice shoots. By noon he had struck up conversations with the people jammed closest to him. He surprised them with his Chinese, horrible accent and all.

Before this trip, much of what Bill had experienced was thoroughly westernized. However, being totally immersed in Chinese life exceeded anything he had bargained for. Before the first day was over, he remembered it was April Fool's Day. He decided the joke was on him.

People in the western provinces were only beginning to feel the pinch on food. The traveler with money had no problem exploring China's finest foods. Bill enjoyed trying crispy yellow fish, crackling with hot sweet-and-sour sauce; melons steamed to perfection with bits of ham, cabbage, and chicken; bamboo shoots; pigeon eggs; and Peking duck. After a while, though, Bill decided he'd had all the good Chinese food he could eat. He decided to stick to rice!

Two days out of Wuzhou, he entered

Mandarin-speaking country. He could no longer speak in Cantonese. He could read Mandarin and get along fairly well. He loved the people and the sights, sounds, and smells. What might seem a lonely vacation turned into an exotic journey for the young doctor.

Bill began to recuperate from the exhausting routine he had followed the past year. He enjoyed the traditional, colorful life of the Chinese and all the country had to offer.

When Bill arrived in Chongqing, he went to one of the flourishing mission hospitals there and made contact with another missionary doctor. Though they had never met before, they became fast friends. They spent a few days together, touring the city, talking about their work, and learning from one another.

The doctor gave Bill an insider's view of the city. Bill saw the results of drug trafficking and many diseases. The doctor showed him some of the competition for his healing art. Herb doctors mysteriously mixed weird recipes, calling for everything from children's urine to musk crystals. Also, a live rooster bound to the chest of a corpse would do wonders in keeping away evil spirits.

As they walked down the old streets, dodging squealing pigs and squawking hens, Bill asked his friend the question he was struggling with. "How do you ever get used to the idea that you are going to be able to make such a small impression upon all this suffering, even in a lifetime?"

His friend smiled. "You're tackling a problem that almost did me in my first term of service. I believe every missionary faces it. It's a kind of crisis of compassion. You can either narrow your eyes against it and harden your heart—and all of us do that to a degree—or you can let it drive you to a pace that will break you. Those are the extreme reactions, of course. I finally had to face the fact that God is fully aware of my limitations, and He brought me here for a purpose. I must do what my hand finds to do to the best of my ability. But, I must leave the statistics up to God, even as I have to leave the course of history up to him."

Bill said gloomily, "I am more aware of my limitations than I have ever been. I guess my problem is that I have been imposing my limitations on God."

"Each of us has to make this adjustment by himself," his friend said. "Some never do. It's a time when a missionary's faith is tried to its foundation and his emotional strength is tested to its core."

Bill thought about his friend's words for a long time. From Chongqing, Bill went to Chengdu, a great university center, soon to be the center of most of the great universities of China. Here he saw East and West in contrast. Women dressed in the latest Western fashions walked beside others in traditional Chinese fashions. Many women hobbled down the street with tiny, deformed feet. This was the result of an ancient tradition called foot-binding. The Chinese considered small feet a sign of beauty.

Bill spent nearly a week in Chengdu. He visited the universities and the hospitals.

He met with missionaries and studied new techniques in surgery. Some methods developed at this time in China were unique and untried elsewhere in the world.

Despite his shyness, Bill liked meeting people and learning from them. After spending time with him, people were amazed at how much they had talked and how little he had talked and how little they had noticed that.

After a week, Bill said goodbye to his new friends at Chengdu. He boarded a colorful river steamer to travel down the mighty Yangtze River to Hankou. The Japanese were preparing an offensive against Hankou, but at the time Bill booked his ship, the floods from the Yellow River had slowed them down. Bill decided to see this remarkably industrialized city while he had the chance. It took him two more weeks to get from Hankou through the Hunan Province back into Guangxi.

Totally caught up in his adventure, Bill had not kept in touch with the people at Wuzhou. As a result, Dr. Beddoe was worried when he had gotten no word from Bill after five weeks. He wrote Dr. Maddry earlier and told him he thought it was unwise for Bill to go, but he pointed out there was no stopping him. Bill's pleasant stubbornness often frustrated Dr. Beddoe.

Bill and Dr. Beddoe still did not understand each other, but they both respected each other. Bill's shyness around people in charge only made the problem worse. One of the remarkable stories of Bill's life is the way he gradually won Dr. Beddoe's confidence.

Through the years, the administrator saw his young colleague develop and demonstrate some of the very characteristics he felt Bill so lacked.

In the middle of May 1938, Bill arrived back in Wuzhou. He was refreshed and enthusiastic. He was more at peace than at any time since coming to China.

Chapter 18: Bombings Continue

The city was bombed for the third time in two weeks after Bill returned from vacation. A week later the plane that flew between Hong Kong and Chongqing, making a regular stop at Wuzhou, was shot down just south of the city. Its escaping passengers were machine-gunned to their deaths. Up to this time, the staff of Stout Memorial Hospital felt the Japanese would not intentionally bomb them. On the roof they painted a gigantic American flag and on either side of it huge crosses.

All feeling of security disappeared September 17, 1938. The siren sounded its eerie warning at midmorning. Bill was involved in a delicate, extremely dangerous stomach surgery. When the operating team heard the siren, they froze for an instant. Then, they turned to look at the surgeon.

Bill's voice was muffled by his mask. His tone was calm and authoritative. "Miss Luk, Dr. Leung, stay with me. The rest of you help the staff get the patients to the basement; then go there yourselves."

"But Waa I Saang, the Japanese?"

"Do what I say. We are not finished here, and we certainly cannot stop."

Beads of sweat glistened on his forehead. Miss Luk sponged his head; the operation went on.

They were almost finished when they heard the planes. First a drone, the high whine of dive bombers. Unconsciously, Bill spread his feet. He braced himself against the expected concussion. He was closing the incision, stitching quickly. Again, he looked up. "You go now. They will need you."

"But, Doctor, what about you and the patient?"

"I will move him into the ward at the end of the hall where the windows have not been replaced. It will be less dangerous."

His last words were all but lost as explosions came. Some were dull and thudding, as if at a great distance. Others were earsplitting and very close. "Go! Hurry!" It was a command.

Outside the hospital, terror reigned. In back alleys and along tiny streets dozens of men, women, and children were killed by raging fires. Up wide streets red tracer bullets left behind twisted remnants of life. In the few shelters the living huddled on top of those crushed to death in the panic. Inside the hospital courtyard, hundreds of Chinese crouched. They hoped the American flag and the red crosses on top of the great building would provide safety.

Shortly after the first bombs fell, Bill finished his surgery. He rolled his patient into the big ward on the top floor. His choice was simple. The patient could not be moved downstairs, and there was some protection here because all the glass had been broken. As the patient came back to consciousness, Bill leaned over him to hold him on the bed. He tried to reassure him in his Tennessee-accented Cantonese.

Then the Japanese attacking force turned on the hospital compound. Nineteen bombs exploded within the supposedly neutral area dedicated to mercy. The building shook as if it would disintegrate. One of the bombs landed on the roof immediately over the place where Bill hovered with his patient. The explosion sent plaster and debris everywhere. It left a gaping hole in the roof, and the chair, bed, doctor, and patient were flung across the floor. By God's mercy, neither Bill nor his patient was injured. With that final act, the planes departed.

As soon as the planes left, the staff members rushed from the basement to the top floor. There they found Bill and the patient praying together—a stumbling, poorly phrased, but thoroughly sincere prayer. When the staff saw Bill and his patient safe, they cried with joy! They all knelt to give their own prayers of thanksgiving.

Bill's bravery would have won the Medal of Honor if he were a soldier on the battlefield. God does not have ceremonies in this life for

His heroes, but the Bible tells of a time to come when the heavens will take note. The legend of Bill Wallace was taking shape.

The wounded began to pour into the hospital. They were coming up the hill. Some were carried on broken doors, charred boards, and even in baskets. For Bill and his staff, it was the beginning of a nightmare that refused to end. They cut, clamped, and stitched those who were hurting. They groaned when lives were lost and celebrated when people recovered.

The waiting room looked like a slaughter house. The bruised and bleeding bodies of men, women, and children were everywhere. Every bed in the hospital held a victim. Up and down the corridors suffering people of all ages and all sizes lay helpless, groaning, and dying.

Later, the exhausted, hollow-eyed doctor stood in his red-stained white operating coat, looking over the city of Wuzhou. A third of it had been destroyed. Thousands of people were homeless, hungry, or dead. He remembered his Chongqing friend's advice. "You do what you are able to do, and you leave the statistics to the Lord."

The next morning the missionaries set up a soup kitchen in front of the clinic. They served rice soup with a few sparse vegetables. A cable to the American consul told of the bombing. A strong diplomatic protest was relayed to Tokyo. It did little good.

Dr. Bill Wallace's trial term was becoming a trial by fire.

Chapter 19: Guangzhou Falls

Eugene Hill stood on the Guangzhou dock watching the passengers unload from the West River steamer. In a moment he spotted the man he was meeting. Tall and smiling and dressed in a white suit, Bill sprang to the dock and warmly greeted his friend. Gene noted that Bill's energy didn't match the experience of the past few months, except for his eyes. They were more mature. Bill had a new toughness about him—war will do that to a man.

"Well, Doctor, I expected you to stay up there in your nice, safe Guangxi retreat," Gene said as he greeted Bill. "There's a war down here, you know."

"I was dying from boredom, and I had to have some excitement," Bill laughed. He was happy to see his old friend.

Gene laughed. "Seriously, when the Japanese landed at Bias Bay last week, I thought surely Dr. Beddoe would forbid you to come to the executive meeting."

"Well," Bill admitted with a grin, "he wasn't exactly enthusiastic about it."

Gene replied, "He knows what a stubborn surgeon he has, and he has probably resigned himself to it with good Christian grace." He laughed and gave Bill a friendly slap on the back.

"The executive committee business is a rather important honor," Bill said. "I'm not going to let the Japanese do me out of it."

"What do you mean, 'honor'? They elected us to the committee because they knew we were foolish enough to come to a meeting like this, bombings and all."

Laughing together, they climbed into rickshaws for the ride to Gene's home where Bill would stay. As they rode along, Gene explained the situation.

"Bill, I came within an inch of telegraphing you today to tell you not to come. We thought we would have plenty of time to meet and finish our business in time for you to get back home. I am not so sure now. The Japanese landed at Bias Bay, and their tanks are moving across the rice fields, which are rock hard, thanks to the drought. They are meeting very little resistance. Unless the Chinese can regroup within the next day or two, nothing can stop them from rolling in here later this week."

Bill gave a soft whistle. "I didn't realize they could get here that fast. I thought it would be at least another ten days." He paused and then asked, "What about Louise? Isn't she expecting a baby pretty soon?"

Gene was serious. "Yes, she is. I tried to get her to go out to Hong Kong, but she is even more stubborn than a certain doctor I know."

"She's just afraid to leave you," Bill kidded. "She knows you wouldn't know what to do without her."

"Man, that's closer to the truth than you realize!" exclaimed Gene. "But I do have a plan. I have rented an apartment on Sha-Mein and Dr. Hayes has agreed to look after her. She should be safe there."

Bill nodded. Sha-Mein was a neutral area separated from Guangzhou proper by a narrow canal about fifty feet wide. So far, the Japanese had not attacked neutral zones. The missionaries thought they probably would honor Sha-Mein, too.

"That's a good idea, Gene. I think she will be better off there," Bill said. "But what are you going to do about the seminary?"

Gene was a professor at Graves Theological Seminary. The seminary stood on a hill at the edge of Guangzhou.

"We are dismissing classes Wednesday, and the Chinese faculty and students are leaving immediately," Gene said. "If the Chinese resist right into the city, that seminary is not going to be a very safe place. The hospital is closing, too. The patients have been either dismissed or sent up the river. Most of the medical staff will go up country or to Hong Kong."

Bill said, "I am surprised to see so many people and cars still in the streets. I would have thought the bombings would bring this place to a standstill."

"It gets quiet quickly," said Gene. "A small flight came over early this morning. You can see some smoke over to the left at this next corner. That's where most of the bombs hit. They are government buildings."

"Well, one thing is certain," Bill said grimly. "This will be one of the shortest executive committee meetings in the history of the South China Mission."

"It will be if I have anything to do with it," said Gene.

And it was. By the second afternoon all the emergency decisions before the executive committee had been made. Letters, telegrams, and cablegrams were sent. Just before the meeting adjourned, a large flight of Japanese bombers hit Guangzhou. The committee's meeting place in Dr. Hayes' office on Sha-Mein was not hit, but the explosions around them and the sound of machine gun bullets scared those at the meeting.

Now the problem for the members of the committee was how to get out. Alec Herring, one of the executive committee members, went to Hong Kong on a Standard Oil launch. Bill decided to wait until early the next morning to try to get a boat to Wuzhou.

The next morning, Bill worked his way through the masses of people jamming streets that led to the main bridge out of Guangzhou. He finally reached the docks. He might as well have been trying to go to the moon. Not even a small boat was available. The regular boats had canceled, and foreign gunboats had pulled out to safety.

As he stood looking at the scene, he wondered how he would get back to his hospital in Wuzhou. Just then, air raid sirens tore through the morning air. People rushed for shelter. Bill watched the planes roar into the harbor area. Red tracer bullets cut their way into boat after boat, leaving them in flames. With a start, he realized they were now spitting their fire at him! He barely made the shelter of some freight boxes before the dock he was standing on was splintered by machine gun fire. Now he decided he did not need to go home that badly! Running hard and low, he started back to the Hills' house.

When Gene and his wife returned from the seminary, they found Bill lying casually across a bed. Raising himself up on one elbow, he grinned and said, "You know, a guy could get killed out there."

Gene was not amused. "The latest news bulletin says the Japanese are just ten miles away. That means they are going to get here sometime tomorrow. You may be permanently assigned to this area by the Japanese."

Louise Hill, ever cheerful, quickly whipped up a lunch. Soon they were relaxed, despite the uncertainty. Later that afternoon, Gene finally convinced Louise to go to Sha-Mein. He borrowed the hospital car and moved her to the apartment there.

The roar of guns and the incessant whine of airplanes woke Bill and Gene before daylight the next morning. They drove to Sha-Mein to check on Louise and to see if they could find Bill a way back to Wuzhou. The docks were deserted. No boats could be seen anywhere on the river. Bill had a funny feeling in the pit of his stomach. He realized he was not going anywhere.

To the northeast, the roar of big guns grew louder. In the distance they could see an occasional flash of fire as the battle moved toward the city.

After watching the scene a moment, Bill said to Gene with a sigh, "Well, I guess this is obvious enough. Let's try to get back and see if we can help those people who are taking refuge in the hospital."

When they reached the hospital, they realized it was one of the safest places in the city. Its subbasement was a bomb shelter. It would also protect those there from crossfire. Quickly, they formed a plan. The hospital basement could serve as a refugee center, but they must act immediately.

After arranging the subbasement to take care of about fifty people, Gene, Bill, and Dr. F. D. Woodward, who was also present for the executive committee meeting, moved through the community. They enlisted the Christians there to help them gather their people and bring them to the hospital. The Chinese were urged to bring all the food they had and extra clothes and to get to the hospital immediately.

Then, somehow, the Chinese knew the lines had broken and the Japanese would soon be in their city. Panic set in! Thousands of people started a great rush out of the burning city. The crush stopped the missionaries' progress. They took shelter in a side street and waited for the stampeding crowd to clear. They witnessed one of the most horrible sights they had ever seen. In their panic, people began to trample one another in the headlong rush from the bombs.

After a lull, Bill and Gene took off in the hospital car. Soon they were stopped by the crowds. Gunfire from a Japanese plane cleared the street for a moment. Bill wheeled the car across the thoroughfare and past the congestion. Their drive back to the hospital was a hair-raising experience! They finally decided to leave the car a couple of blocks away since it was such an easy target for machine guns. They had little time left, so they started toward the Hills' home for bedding and supplies. As they passed the seminary, they saw it was now an armed bastion. A battle was being fought there. A Chinese rear-guard group had commandeered the area to harass the oncoming Japanese forces. The Japanese were, in turn, pouring a withering fire into the little campus. As the missionaries watched, they saw several Chinese defenders topple over.

Quickly, Bill and Gene went around the campus. They took a low and sheltered road back to the Hills' house where a supply of canned food still lay untouched. At the Hills' house, they chucked four baskets full of canned goods into some bed sheets. Then, gathering up their bundles, they started for the hospital. Gene was a strapping 200-pound man. He had no trouble picking up his load and starting down the street. Bill was a little over 140 pounds. He had to abandon half his load before he got far. Praying the Japanese forces had not taken the seminary campus yet, they ran down the streets.

As the two missionaries trotted under their heavy loads, they crossed the street below the seminary. They could see the Chinese soldiers abandoning their positions. When they reached an open square they had to cross to get to the hospital, the missionaries saw people running back and forth across the area to find last minute shelter. They heard the rumble of Japanese tanks. They also heard the screams of people, the crackle of fire, and the whine of the overhead planes.

A Chinese running across the square spotted them. He called Gene by name and ran toward them. "Pastor Hill! Pastor Hill, save my life!" Ten feet away the man staggered and fell, dead. Within a few seconds a dozen people had fallen in front of the horror-stricken missionaries. Then they realized what was happening. They had stopped at the corner and were sheltered from a tank coming down the street to their right. There was no hope of getting back to the hospital now. Bill turned to Gene and said, "Let's turn back. We're going to get killed!"

Their conversation as they retraced their steps didn't show their fear. "Don't you want to go to heaven?" Gene asked.

The panting doctor replied, "Yes, but I didn't expect to get there today."

As they reached Gene's house, they dumped their packs in the hallway. They dove for a nook behind the hall steps, squeezing themselves as close to the floor as they could get.

No sooner had they taken cover than Japanese tanks, crunching through the streets, sprayed machine gun bullets against the house. The exploding shells from the rumbling tanks and the falling bombs shook loose the plaster. It showered the two missionaries huddled on the floor.

After a moment's lull, Bill raised his head and whispered, "Gene, you all right? Do you think it is safe for us to go to the hospital?"

"I don't know. I'm afraid to look."

"I'm going to take a look," Bill said. On all fours he crawled down the entrance hall to the shattered door. He gently pulled it back and peeked down the street. The rumble of another tank and a din of fire greeted him. Scrambling, he barely had returned to his shelter before another burst was fired into the residence. This time he and Gene lay there for a full fifteen minutes before either dared speak, much less move. Days later, they counted thirty-eight bullet holes in the house.

Cautiously, Gene moved to the door. The street was quiet and deserted. He said to his friend, "If we're ever going to get to the hospital, we've got to go now."

Again they shouldered their loads and started into the streets. The roar of still another tank convinced them they would never make it. There was nothing to do except drop the food and run.

Bill said, "Let's go! Every man for

himself!"

Gene and Bill later wished they had timed the quarter-mile they ran from Gene's house to the hospital. Dodging the square this time, Gene turned the last corner before reaching the hospital. He paused for a moment to look back. Bill was nowhere in sight. Panic seized the seminary teacher. He started to return, sure that his friend had been caught in the withering crossfire. Just as he did, he saw Bill come around the corner, running for all he was worth, his arms flailing the air. Shells were hitting behind him, grazing the corner, but he was safe!

When the two arrived at the hospital, they found 268 refugees packed in the basement. Soon the wounded civilians and soldiers began pouring in. Some were walking. Others were carried by friends or fellow soldiers. All were stripped to their underwear so the Japanese would not recognize them as soldiers and shoot them. The suffocating smells included the odor of fear and the stench of torn flesh and dried blood. As Bill got his breath, he took charge of the wounded. With meager supplies, he began treating them. Most were suffering from shrapnel wounds. It was a bloody job.

Outside the hospital, Japanese tanks cruised back and forth broadcasting orders in Cantonese. They told the people to stay out of sight. Anyone in the streets would be shot. Bill, not bothering to look up from his work, said, "He's not going to have to tell me twice!"

As he worked, Gene suddenly appeared

at his side. "Where have you been?" asked Bill.

"I went upstairs to see if I could make a telephone call." Bill looked at him to see if he had gone mad. "I took a chance that the line was not yet down. I got a call in to the United Press office."

"What did they say?"

"They asked me how it was out here. When I said that the Japanese tanks were roaming the streets, they replied, 'Then it's all over. Guangzhou has fallen.'"

It was Friday, October 21, 1938, 3:08 p.m.

Outside, unchecked fires lit up the night sky. Inside, Bill worked by flashlight to ease as much suffering as he could. Toward morning he decided he would have to operate on a young woman. Gene managed to get a set of instruments from the operating room upstairs under cover of darkness. They would have to wait for morning's light to do the surgery. Sadly, just before sunrise her life ebbed away. Bill bowed his head and sobbed with fatigue and sorrow.

The two men stayed in their basement shelter Saturday and Sunday. When they came out on Monday, the smell of death was everywhere. Few bodies had been removed. Boldly approaching the first Japanese soldiers, they showed their credentials and were allowed to pass.

The next day Bill went to the American consulate. He arranged passage on a British gunboat that was leaving for Wuzhou on Wednesday. Over the next two days, he and

Gene worked to get the hospital into shape for greater use.

An hour after Bill boarded the HMS Robin on Wednesday, the Japanese imposed a curfew on the city, which would have prevented Bill from leaving.

As the Robin steamed out of Guangzhou harbor, Bill gave a big sigh. For nearly a week, he had not stopped to think about Wuzhou or Knoxville or anything but the next moment and the work at hand. He had not even thought to notify the hospital that he was all right.

The entire staff of the Stout Memorial Hospital were worried about Bill. In the hospital chapel they prayed for their friend. An hour later Dr. Beddoe received a message from Bill:

```
Arriving tomorrow on
Robin. WALLACE.
```

Chapter 20: Things Get Worse

Bill stood on the porch of the hospital sipping an early morning cup of coffee. Sooner or later he was going to have to get some sleep. There did not seem to be a place to stop. Every bed was filled. The emergency ward they had set up in the basement was dangerously overcrowded.

He saw Dr. Beddoe come out of the clinic. He had a stethoscope in one hand and a bulging clipboard in the other. His sleeves were rolled up past his elbows. His collar was loose. It occurred to Bill that he did not often see Dr. Beddoe that informal. Bill also noticed how tired he looked.

"I wonder if I'll ever smile again," the superintendent said absently as he wiped the sweat under his collar with a handkerchief. "Refugees keep coming and coming. I would not be surprised if ten thousand had come through here since Guangzhou fell."

"I think we have most of them in the

hospital," Bill said.

"I'm sure it seems like it," Dr. Beddoe replied. Then he handed Bill the clipboard.

"We are going to have to find room for at least ten more," he said. "They can only survive with hospital treatment. We are treating and turning away people we would normally hospitalize."

Taking the clipboard, Bill said, "I'll see if we can clear ten more beds. There isn't room for more pallets." Finishing his coffee, he started back into the hospital, then stopped and said, "When was it last normal around here?"

Dr. Beddoe shrugged. "I'm not sure I can remember." He looked down at the crowded clinic. He saw a nurse frantically waving to get his attention. He added, "The sights I have seen since then will take care of my nightmares for years to come."

Shortly after Bill returned from Guangzhou, Dr. Beddoe called his staff together to consider the emergency. Japanese occupation was now a definite threat. Dr. Beddoe shared some of the things Bill had seen in Guangzhou. He told them he would understand if they chose to leave. They each assured him they would stay. The old missionary broke down in tears. He was very touched by their commitment.

But staying proved to be very difficult. Usually a crisis lasted for a while, but eventually it passed. This crisis, brought on by the many, many refugees, had no ending. The hospital was unable to keep accurate records with the large number of refugees. No one could remember how many operations Bill performed day and night. He grew very thin. At night the soft lights of the hospital reflected on his blood-spattered white coat. He moved quietly through the crowded wards, taking care of the more serious patients, ordering medication for others, and examining others in preparation for surgery the next day.

With their sulfa and bandages, Bill, Dr. Beddoe, and the nurses also shared the good news of Jesus Christ. The hospital evangelists and their helpers conducted daily services. Again and again, patients found hope and life through Jesus.

Bill was a doctor. His basic ministry was making sick people well. But he was in China first of all to share the good news of Jesus Christ. He brought a message of forgiveness and eternal life through God's love and grace. Sometimes his soft witness to that grace was more effective than even the best preacher's sermon.

When Bill and Dr. Beddoe discussed how much longer their supplies and their physical strength could last, they realized things were changing. The Japanese were not advancing from Guangzhou. With the strategic pocket around that city, they seemed content. They had control of all of China's industrial centers and leading ports as well as the main arteries of commerce. The three areas where foreign, economic, and commercial interests were heaviest were in their hands. The great river systems were now controlled by their forces of nearly one million men. But the

Chinese held on.

Chapter 21: Bill Gets Another Job

With a brief break from the war, Bill now faced a job he did not want. Dr. and Mrs. Beddoe had worked at Wuzhou for six years with almost no break. They needed time in the United States to rest and recover. Bill would have to serve as superintendent of the hospital for a year during 1939.

Dr. Beddoe had come to the hospital at a time of crisis. He had done an excellent job of building the hospital into a source of help for many people. Now, Bill was also recognized as a great surgeon throughout South China. Thanks to him, the people who had once looked on the hospital suspiciously and called the missionaries, "Foreign Devils," were looking with pride on the Christian hospital. They called it "The Life of China."

All the misgivings Dr. Beddoe had about Dr. Wallace's administrative abilities were focused on preparing to leave China. He left no stone unturned to make sure the hospital was self-sufficient. He set up a group of business managers and dismissed the student nurses. He reorganized the graduate nurses, ordered supplies for months ahead, and tried to anticipate every decision that Bill might face during the time he would be left in charge. Finally, saying goodbye to Bill and to Rex Ray, the only Southern Baptist missionaries left in Wuzhou, Dr. and Mrs. Beddoe left for Hong Kong, the United States, and Texas. While Bill did not voice his feelings too often, he admitted 1939 was going to be a hard year. He was chief of staff, charged with a resident program, carrying a backbreaking surgery schedule, and now, hospital administrator.

Bill still had not learned to delegate responsibility. Soon the surprised staff realized that Bill would do the work himself rather than ask someone else. Whether it was a plumbing fixture, a door hinge, or a complicated X-ray piece, Bill would fix it. He liked to work this way. The mechanic in him came to the front. Things didn't run the way Dr. Beddoe might have liked, but the hospital work went on. In fact, it did well.

One day, Bill came up as a hospital nurse was arguing with two orderlies about removing a body. The orderlies were highly superstitious, and they thought the work was beneath them. They refused to do the work. Bill caught the drift of the conversation, picked up the body in his arms, and walked past the open-mouthed orderlies to the morgue. It was the last time a Stout Memorial orderly ever refused to carry a body. If the great doctor could do this, surely it was not beneath them! Drawn by Bill's humility and dedication, the Chinese followed him in a way which allowed the hospital to do excellent work.

Bill worked hard that year to carry on all his assignments. Somebody wrote to Dr. Maddry in Richmond that Bill was at a breaking point. No one knows who made the statement. Dr. Maddry became so concerned he immediately wired Dr. Beddoe, who was speaking in Florida. He asked him to check the story and prepare to return to China at the earliest possible moment.

Two weeks later Dr. Beddoe received the longest letter he ever received from Bill:

> Everything is going along peacefully in Wuzhou. I expect when you get this letter, you will be packing up to come back. We certainly need you. I am a bad manager and a bad financier. I am afraid you did not get much satisfaction from my list of drugs, but it is very hard to say what you need for a year in advance. However, the list we sent you constitutes the main drugs in amounts we used this year. It'll be a good idea to bring some rubber gloves, hot water

```
bottles, and sheets also.
Perhaps in light of some
inquiries, I should also
say I have never felt
better or been happier in
my whole life than I am
right now.
```

Another letter from one of the office workers and still another one from Rex Ray confirmed that Bill was not only holding up well, but he was actually thriving. Bill was happiest meeting the needs of people and doing the work he felt called to do. The busier and more demanding the work, the greater his sense of fulfillment. Though he felt the strain of five long years in China, he was definitely in his element.

Dr. Beddoe found the hospital full and prospering when he returned to Wuzhou in July 1940. Except for the growing problem of supplies, due to the Japanese blockade, the hospital stood strong and sure. It was obvious to Dr. Beddoe that Bill had done a magnificent job.

Now it was Bill's time to return to the United States. The hospital staff hated to see him go when he was so desperately needed. But, they realized his plans to spend a year in advanced surgical studies would make him even more valuable to the Stout Memorial Hospital.

Several colleagues wrote to the Board shortly after he left for the States, expressing their appreciation of him. Their letters told what kind of trial term the young missionary had had:

> There is no overstating the value of Dr. Wallace's work. No words of mine could over-praise him.
>
> Dr. Wallace has a brilliant future in China. His fame will travel over an entire nation, a distinction he could hardly expect to attain in America.
>
> He might be called Silent Bill, for he is a man of few words, but brave deeds. Words may vanish into thin air, but deeds never die. It was the deed on the Cross that saved the world.
>
> What Dr. Wallace did during his first term of service in China—the trial term—will bear fruit down through the years.
>
> As a physician he possesses, to a greater

```
degree than any man I
have ever known, the first
requisite—that of staying
by the job at hand till
the heavens fall and
though all hope seems to
be lost.

If you want to find him,
find the sickest patient
in the hospital, and
there he will be.
```

Bill Wallace was unaware of the praise.
He was heading home. The blue of the Pacific
Ocean and the peaceful nights at sea turned his
thoughts from his adopted country to his native
land. His thoughts were now of Knoxville and
friends and the Tennessee hills. He looked
forward to a year of study and renewed
friendships. His trial term was behind him. He
had already evaluated it and summed it up:

```
When I get back home, I
don't know how I will
stack up as far as my
profession is concerned.
Had I been in America, I
could always have gone to
an older doctor and asked
him how to do certain
operations, but I was the
only surgeon there. No,
I don't know how I will
stack up as far as my
```

profession is concerned,
but I can say this, I
know the Lord Jesus
Christ better than I did
five years ago.

Chapter 22: Bill Visits the United States

The countryside flashed by the window as the train rumbled east toward Tennessee. Mountains, desert, canyons, plains, and woods took their turn onstage. Bill drank it in. He was excited to be back in the United States.

He noticed that his clothes were out of style. Snatches of conversation convinced him he was going to need to relearn the language. Even the expressions people used had changed. He laughed out loud at the words of a popular song. The scene was both strange and familiar. The sights and smells of China were fading. The present consumed his thinking. In his mind's eye he was seeing Knoxville and Broad Street, the old home place, and his sister, Ruth Lynn and her husband, Syd. They were becoming clear again after having been so dim through the years in China.

"What makes a doctor spend his life in a place like China?" His dinner companion's question brought him back to the moment.

"Don't misunderstand me; I admire you for it. I just wonder why."

Bill smiled, "I guess each person's reasoning is unique, but my reason is simple enough. When I was trying to decide what I should do with my life, I became convinced that God wanted me to be a medical missionary. That decision took me to China. And that, along with the fact that I was extremely happy there, will take me back." He paused for a moment, a little uneasy before his companion's obvious admiration. "I'm not going back because I'm heroic. Actually, I'm a coward. But I want to go back because it's where I'm supposed to be."

The man, a successful business executive, was silent, lost in his own thoughts. Then, turning to the candid, clear-eyed missionary, he said, "You make me wonder if I have not missed something down the line."

"Knoxville! Knoxville!" The familiar cry of the conductor was unnecessary. For two hours Bill had been aware of the East Tennessee countryside. He loved each scene. He noticed the new things and remembered the old.

Then he was home. Ruth Lynn and Syd Stegall were there to greet him. For a few moments they all talked at once, laughing and happy to be together again.

On the way home, Bill had them drive him around Knoxville so he could see the city and the way it had changed. The cars enthralled him. The magazines had kept him up-to-date on most model changes, but here they were, sleek and shiny, all of them.

They drove by the old home on the corner of Broadway and Silver and stopped across the street. Bill just looked. A lot of memories rushed back. He wished for a moment he could see patients walking into the downstairs entrance, or the lean figure of his father emerge with candy for a child, stethoscope dangling from his neck. The nostalgia was strong, but it made him aware of how much time had passed since his departure five years earlier.

Bill's brother-in-law had built a new home on the north side of Knoxville. It was to become Bill's "permanent address." He loved the place, with its big trees and broad, sloping lawn. He especially loved the brick patio and barbecue pit. He claimed a breezeway for himself and called it a sleeping porch. That evening they sat under the trees and talked.

At first Ruth Lynn and Sydney asked Bill lots of questions. Soon, though, they found themselves doing the talking. They filled Bill in on things that had happened while he was gone. He had turned the conversation away from himself.

Two days later he was walking the wooded slopes of the Smoky Mountains near Gatlinburg. Memories can become exhausted over the years. As he walked, he realized he needed to refuel for the years ahead. With senses alert, he took in the haze of the mountains, the green of the hickories, the laurel, the stately pines, and the broadleaf maples. The bright, sparkling waters of the creeks splashing across the rocks lifted his spirits.

Everyone wanted to see him. Friends and relatives invited him for dinner. They unsuccessfully tried to get him to talk about China and the bombings and the war. They ended up talking about themselves and what they had done during the last five years.

The chief bane of his time in the U.S. was that everyone wanted him to speak. He declared he would rather go through a Japanese air raid than do so. He knew people wanted him to relive his experiences. It was difficult for him even to share the basic facts. The blood, destruction, hunger, and suffering of China were a long way off. He was not one to live in the past. China's needs continued to live in his daily prayers, but he had laid them aside for the present.

Bill did make two speeches. The first one was to a woman's group. One day before the meeting, Ruth Lynn peered out of her kitchen window and saw him walking back and forth over the green yard. He was agonizing over what he would say. From time to time he leaned against a tree and, with painfully self-conscious gestures, mumbled the words of his tediously prepared speech. No one was more aware than Bill that when God passed out gifts, public speaking was not one of his. He managed to dodge most speech-making. At church he got away with just speaking to people individually and smiling at them. They did all the talking.

Bill realized that his time in the U.S. was a time for renewal, but he also saw it as a

God-given opportunity to sharpen his skills as a surgeon.

He originally planned to study in Europe. The war and Nazi aggression put an end to that. He read his medical journals avidly, even in China. From his reading, he decided that the University of Pennsylvania's postgraduate course in surgery would be the best investment of his time. He had asked Sydney to enroll for him even before he returned to the States. He also realized he could take another short course in X-ray at Harvard University when he completed his work at the University of Pennsylvania.

September found Bill hard at work in the University of Pennsylvania's postgraduate course in surgery. He settled into his new surroundings and enjoyed the scientific atmosphere. Like a starving man, he launched himself into intensive study. He took only a few short vacations for sightseeing and to visit friends. He spent most of his free time observing surgery, browsing through the vast medical archives, and discussing new techniques with more experienced surgeons. More than once, as he worked or heard a lecture or observed an operation, a scene from China would return to his mind. He would think of a patient that he could now help. He would quietly thank God for his opportunity.

Bill finished his work in Philadelphia in late spring. After a brief visit in Knoxville, he traveled by train to Boston and Harvard, where he began his special studies. Again, he was thrilled with the opportunity to work in an advanced medical center with some of the most brilliant minds in medicine.

He remembered his old friend Dr. Dewey Peters's admonition, "Always practice the best medicine." Because of these opportunities, Bill realized he would be able to practice a lot better medicine when he returned to Wuzhou.

He finished his study at Harvard and realized it was time to return to China. He had time for a few days in Knoxville. Then he would leave for San Francisco, provided his visa and passage came through. Soon, he would be on his way back to China.

Chapter 23: Bill Returns to China

Dr. Beddoe was worried. He knew Bill had set sail from San Francisco August 14 and had arrived in Hong Kong September 3. It was now almost three weeks past the time Bill should have arrived in Wuzhou. By October 3 Bill still had not arrived. At a hospital chapel service October 6, the staff prayed for Bill's safe arrival. The staff was so concerned that one of the nurses cried out during the prayer time, "He is dead! I know he is dead!" Gloom was settling over the waiting staff.

The next day a dusty American climbed painfully from a pedicab in front of the Baptist clinic. As the driver shuffled off with his rickety vehicle, the man stood for a moment, looking at the clinic and the hospital that towered behind it. He looked like a man drinking in a sight he had not really expected to see again. Then, picking up a worn bag, he walked up the steps. His arrival caused a celebration that rivaled the Chinese New Year.

"Waa I Saang is back!" The cry echoed across the hospital yard. Within seconds, every person in the five-story building had heard the news.

Dr. Beddoe breathed a fervent prayer of thanks. Then he rushed out to greet Bill, though he reminded himself that his surgeon had caused him a lot of anxiety by not wiring his whereabouts. But, when he saw the grinning, slender figure surrounded by laughing, weeping, chattering staff members, he forgot all about his worries. Bill, seeing the blinking administrator, knew he was welcome.

That night at supper Bill talked matter-of-factly of the strange and miraculous journey that brought him back to Wuzhou. With Japanese planes harassing all traffic, and especially railroad traffic, the trains ran only at night, if they ran at all. To get back to Wuzhou, Bill tried bus, train, car, and even walking. More than once he jumped for cover as Japanese planes roared down from the China skies. He related frantic efforts to claw a hole in the mud-and-water-filled ditches to find cover.

Once his train remained in a mountain tunnel all day to avoid Japanese planes that were lying in wait for it. Another time he and his fellow travelers abandoned a bus and ran for cover as Japanese troops cut off the road. The story could have been told heroically, but before Bill had finished, he had his hearers laughing.

Within a few days Bill felt as if he had never left Wuzhou. Caught up in the work, he settled himself into the China scene, warmly aware that he was more comfortable than ever. This was his home.

His reputation as a surgeon did not suffer while he was gone. Soon he began his routine marathon schedule. He was performing operations by 6:30 on most mornings and did not pause for breakfast until around midmorning. Then, he usually ate a piece of bread and drank a glass of milk as he took steps, two at a time, from surgery, to the ward, to his office. He was on call at all times. He often visited the hospital several times during the night. He indulged his patients to a fault, giving them just what was asked unless some principle was involved. He tried always to make sure that every patient received "good medicine."

In the meantime, the stalemate in China was provoking the Japanese to new, bolder moves. Then came Pearl Harbor.

Chapter 24: Doing the Will of God

America was planning to strengthen her island bases in the Pacific, and especially the Philippines, but she had not been able to do it before the Japanese struck at a strategic time. Their far-flung maneuvers met with startling success. Hong Kong, Manila, and Singapore all fell before conquering Japanese armies.

This had an immediate effect on Wuzhou. It reduced the outlets Free China had with the rest of the world. Hong Kong was their closest door and their gateway to the rest of the world. Now Hong Kong was in Japanese hands. Indochina was falling to the Japanese. The Burma Road, connecting what is now Myanmar to Southern China, was a risky and limited corridor.

The closing of Hong Kong brought severe supply problems. Food and medicines were more and more difficult to find. Fortunately, there was nothing the "cowboy missionary" from Texas, Rex Ray, loved more than the adventure of running the Japanese blockade for desperately needed medical supplies. They were not always easy to get, but in countless dangerous and sometimes humorous adventures, Rex came home with the supplies.

Inflation was also a problem. Bill commissioned Rex to find some sulfa drugs at any price. Rex brought back a bottle of 1,000 tablets. Price, $3,250, Hong Kong dollars. When Rex apologized for the high price, Bill said, "Forget it, Rex, that's just money. These tablets mean lives. Remember, there's no price tag on life."

The bombs came as before.

On their way to the shelter another day, one of the women missionaries said to Bill, "I am getting so nervous, I don't know what I'll do."

Bill smiled and said, "We'll do what God wants us to do. It doesn't make any difference what happens to us. The only important thing is that when it does happen, we be found doing the will of God."

Chapter 25: Bill Leads the Hospital

The problems of carrying on missionary work became increasingly difficult. The Foreign Mission Board hoped to lessen the difficulty by asking Dr. Beddoe to take on responsibility as Board representative for the whole area. Also Dr. Beddoe took upon himself the responsibilities of the hospital in Guilin. He soon realized that wearing three hats is no easy job. The only thing to do was to turn his Wuzhou responsibilities over to Bill. He and his family would then move to Guilin.

Bill would not talk about it. Every time Dr. Beddoe brought up the subject, he simply said, "I will not accept the administrative responsibility of this hospital, and that's all there is to it." Dr. Beddoe could not understand Bill's attitude.

It is hard to imagine two more different people than Bill Wallace and Robert Beddoe. Dr. Beddoe was a born administrator. Because he allowed Bill to give himself entirely to medicine, Bill's transition to the mission field had gone smoothly. In turn, Bill deeply loved the Beddoes, regarding them almost as a son regards his parents. As far as communication goes, he was much closer to Mrs. Beddoe. She made sure his housekeeper took good care of him, repairing his shirts, mending his socks, and altering his clothes.

But Bill found it difficult to communicate with Dr. Beddoe. They did much better on a feeling level. They understood each other's attitudes without discussing them. When things were brought into the open, the two men sometimes had trouble. So when Dr. Beddoe approached Bill about taking over the hospital so he could go to Guilin, the surgeon's refusal completely frustrated the older missionary.

The problem was aggravated when Rex Ray moved to Shiuchow and asked Bill to take over the job as station treasurer. Bill absolutely refused. When Dr. Beddoe heard about it, he accused Bill of being unwilling to assume his share of the general mission work. He reminded him that in times like this everybody had to accept extra responsibility.

In the early fall of 1943, Bill, usually the picture of health, began to lose strength. An infected tooth made him sick. He suffered from lack of rest caused by his marathon schedule. Realizing that if Bill became physically disabled, the situation would be tragic, Dr. Beddoe abandoned his idea to move to Guilin. He continued to carry on his work from Wuzhou.

When Bill's health began to improve, Dr.

Beddoe decided to take matters into his own hand. Bill came out of surgery one morning to find Dr. Beddoe supervising the removal of his office from the hospital to his home.

Puzzled, Bill asked, "What's up, Doctor?"

"As of tonight, I am severing all relationship with this hospital. I will carry on my other responsibilities from the house." With that Dr. Beddoe picked up a file of letters and walked right past his surgeon. As an afterthought, he said, "Bill, you can either run this hospital or let it fall apart. I'm doing what I have to do."

From his porch a few moments later, Dr. Beddoe saw Bill walking up the path from the hospital. He looked very concerned. When he entered the room, he said simply to Dr. Beddoe, "I will never accept the responsibility of this hospital as long as you are in China."

Dr. Beddoe was completely taken aback. It cut across all that he knew and believed about his fellow worker. Checking his urge to voice a sharp retort, it occurred to him that maybe he was missing something.

"Bill, I don't understand your attitude. Is it based on reasons that you have not shared with me? Tell me why you feel that way."

"It's hard to put into words, but I see this as your hospital. You built it. You saved it when it was on the brink of financial disaster. You've given your life here. Everyone respects you. The whole tone of the hospital is built around you. I don't believe this hospital should be taken from you."

Dr. Beddoe was amazed. Why had he

not seen it before? Bill felt that the Board was asking him to give up something he wanted to take on responsibilities he did not want. If Bill refused to take them on, the Board would allow Dr. Beddoe to stay. Bill had been thinking of him all along.

"I'm sorry I've been too dumb to see why you didn't want me to go, Bill. The Board's not taking the hospital away from me. I feel this new work is a responsibility I have been uniquely prepared for. I want to take it! After the emergency is over, I can come back to the hospital until time for my retirement. Would you accept the responsibility if we ask the Board to agree to the term 'temporary'?"

Bill brightened. "Why yes! I would accept it under those conditions. I will take over as long as you remain administrator and I am simply temporary superintendent."

Telling his wife about the conversation, Dr. Beddoe broke down. The depth of Bill's loyalty to him was something he had not understood.

With fear and trembling, Bill assumed responsibility of running the complex institution. Despite his experience in 1939, it was difficult work. The war made it worse. When it came to a choice between an administrative matter and a patient's need, the decision was not difficult to make. This did not make things easier, however. Within a few months, Dr. Beddoe wrote the Board's secretary in Richmond,

```
Poor Wallace. He is in a
```

```
half-dozen pots of hot
water already. It may be
necessary to get some
non-medical man to take
over the administration
of the hospital.
```

And they had so many problems at the hospital! Some of the student nurses attended an all-night dancing party! It caused a near riot among the evangelistic workers. They felt all discipline had broken down when Dr. Beddoe left. In the past this would have been handled quickly. Bill acted as if it had never happened.

A few weeks later, Dr. Beddoe received a telegram from Wuzhou. There was a problem in the church, and they wanted him to settle it. Dr. Beddoe decided that Bill needed to handle the problem. He sent a telegram to him with a note,

```
This is your
responsibility now.
```

This was almost too much for Bill. It was hard enough to take over the hospital. He did not want to be responsible for the church in Wuzhou, too! He was not Dr. Beddoe. The sooner people stopped thinking he was, the better off he would be.

This was a difficult time for Bill, but he stuck it out. By early 1944, the hospital staff and the missionaries accepted his leadership. Everyone respected him, and everyone worked well together.

In early 1944, workers at the hospital and members of the church began to tell the people of Wuzhou about Jesus in ways they hadn't done before. Bill helped them. Bill encouraged the people in his church to be leaders, too. As a result, they began to share Jesus with those around them like never before.

Bill also became more involved in the community. He ate meals with people. He joined the Rotary Club. He attended civic functions and participated in civic affairs. This was the new Bill Wallace. People appreciated his advice and good judgment as much as his medical skills.

Bill also made friends with missionaries from other organizations in the area. Dr. William Newbern served with the Christian Missionary Alliance. Since Bill was the only Baptist missionary left at Wuzhou, the Newberns often invited him for Sunday dinner. Sunday mornings after church Bill would hurry to finish his rounds at the hospital. Then he would walk into Wuzhou to buy a chicken to take to Sunday lunch at the Newberns.

The nearby Maryknoll mission was a Catholic group. The group had used the Stout Memorial Hospital for its medical care for a long time, but the Catholic missionaries and the Protestant missionaries were not close. Now, to their surprise, Bill not only treated them when they came to the hospital, but he visited the mission to follow up on their care and well-being. He would not accept pay. As a result, Bill "belonged" to all the missionaries of the area. Despite differences of beliefs, he found unity with them in Christ. The differences seemed minor. God was using Bill to bring unity to His work in Wuzhou.

Chapter 26: Should the Hospital Evacuate?

Daily, Bill listened to his radio set. He wanted to understand how the Japanese were advancing. He plotted their course on a worn map of China. The Japanese had begun an all-out offensive in late spring 1944. It was a last-ditch effort after losing ground in the South Pacific. Their effort threatened to break China.

Bill reviewed the meaning of the marks on his map. He knew unless the Japanese were stopped soon, Wuzhou would be cut off from Free China.

Two weeks later Bill's calculations meant nothing. A Japanese drive out of Guangzhou was moving directly up the West River toward Wuzhou. The major Chinese elements were battling to the north. They were trying to protect the American air bases threatened by the Japanese. The Chinese troops left to defend the Japanese drive coming from the east could only hope to slow the advance. As the only

Baptist missionary left at Wuzhou, Bill was completely responsible for the hospital and all the missionary work. He knew he would have to decide "to be occupied" or to evacuate. He prayed for wisdom.

In Guilin, Dr. Beddoe was now the acting field representative for the Foreign Mission Board. He also realized what the Japanese drive meant. He telegraphed Dr. M. Theron Rankin, who had succeeded Dr. Maddry as the FMB's executive secretary:

```
Evacuate all missionary
personnel.
```

On June 21, 1944, Dr. Rankin cabled Dr. Beddoe to urge all missionaries to return to America on the first available transportation. Those who could not find transportation were to move west immediately. Bill was to evacuate Wuzhou.

When Bill received Dr. Beddoe's instructions, he understood for the first time the crushing weight of responsibility. Since the Japanese drive out of Guangzhou had begun, Wuzhou had been jammed with refugees. Men, women and children were fleeing their homes ahead of the Japanese. The hospital had almost reached its limit. Hospital staff were working around the clock. Almost daily, Japanese planes bombed Wuzhou. The roar of their motors, the scream of falling bombs, the explosions and flames, and red and white tracers arching across the sky were all a part of the daily scene.

To evacuate would mean to run out on the greatest challenge the hospital had ever faced. But to stay? Bill had no stomach for Japanese occupation. He knew too much from the incident in Guangzhou. Also, he could not risk harm to the women on his staff and possible destruction of the valuable medical equipment the people needed so badly. If he tried to stay to the last possible moment, how would he get out? And how could he move that equipment? Calling the staff together, he explained the situation as he saw it. He did not try to hide the danger, but he was quick to point out their vital role. To his deep satisfaction, they agreed that the Stout Memorial Hospital could not leave the scene of the battle. They were willing to stay with him, even to the point of Japanese occupation, if Bill felt they could serve the purpose God had called them to.

Bill hurriedly scribbled a note to Dr. Beddoe. He told Dr. Beddoe they would stay for the time being. Dr. Beddoe was frustrated, but he knew Bill. He telegraphed Dr. Rankin of the plans for the rest of the mission and then said,

```
I believe Dr. Wallace
will stay until and if
the enemy takes the city.
I know nothing I can say
or do will influence his
opinion or actions in the
slightest.
```

But Bill's problems were not all about

the many sick and wounded people. Stout Memorial Hospital was without a director for nurses' training, one of its most fruitful ministries. A month before moving to Guilin, Dr. Beddoe sent numerous requests to the Foreign Mission Board for a missionary nurse. When Bill assumed responsibility for the hospital, he intensified the pleas for a nurse. Whenever he heard of a nurse having to leave another area because of war, he immediately wrote to her, often forgetting to send the Board a copy. When he heard of a nurse in the States who was interested, he wrote directly to her, urging her to come as soon as possible.

Finally, it seemed his persistency and prayers would pay off. Missionary Nurse Lucy Wright had served twenty years in North China until she was driven out by the Japanese in 1940. She volunteered to go to Wuzhou. Though she spoke Mandarin rather than Cantonese, the Board knew her training and understanding of the Chinese would make up for not speaking the local language. Bill literally danced with joy when he heard that Lucy Wright had left the States for Wuzhou. He did not count on the difficulties caused by a global war. It took Lucy eight long months on a slow boat to reach, not China, but India. Using all her powers of persuasion, she arranged to board a military flight to Guizhou. She could get no farther. She lived in an evacuated mission station with several other stranded missionaries. The Japanese advance had cut her off from Wuzhou.

In the meantime, the American consul

was doing everything but ordering Bill to close
the hospital and come out. After receiving a
final order, Bill called his staff together and
asked them again, "What should we do?"

"Stay on!" the staff said. The people of
Wuzhou noticed. All the foreigners had left
their city, but Waa I Saang was still there. The
hospital was still open.

"There can be no real danger as long as
the Baptist hospital stays open," the people told
one another.

In the fall 1943 the governor of the
Guangxi Province had suffered a ruptured
appendix. He almost died. He had been treated
at the government hospital, until the doctors
there recommended he be sent to Bill. Officials
brought him to Stout Memorial Hospital.
After a brilliant piece of surgery, Bill ordered
a cot brought into the governor's room. Bill
personally watched over him and saved the
governor's life.

When the governor recovered, he tried
to give Bill expensive gifts. He even wanted to
reward him in a formal Wuzhou ceremony. Bill
would not accept the gifts or the recognition.
He told the governor he was just doing his job.
His reward was seeing the governor get well.
The governor did not forget Bill.

In July 1944 the people of Wuzhou
began to evacuate the city. The governor heard
of the move and sent three large river barges
and a motor launch to the docks of Wuzhou. He
gave orders to evacuate Dr. Bill Wallace and the
hospital staff. But Bill still refused to abandon
the hospital. Then, the governor ordered his

boats to wait for the doctor, even if they had to wait until the Japanese came. The captains were to let nothing drive them from their wait for Bill and the hospital staff.

Above left: Bill Wallace.
Above right: Bill with his dog, Duchess.
Below: Bill Wallace operating, Stout Memorial Hospital.
Right top: Stout Memorial Hospital.
Right bottom: Bill builds an oven while Lucy Wright
(center) and others watch.

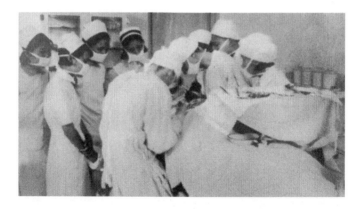

All photos courtesy of the IMB.

All photos courtesy of the IMB.

Chapter 27: A New Plan

Bill now struggled with his decision to stay in Wuzhou. He watched his staff work long hours, to the point of exhaustion and illness. The Japanese bombs would not leave them alone. The conditions became more and more dangerous. He asked himself over and over again, "Am I doing the right thing?" Finally, taking a chance he could get one more cable out, he wired Dr. Rankin, asking advice. Dr. Rankin was sensitive to Bill's struggle. He replied,

```
We can't advise, but we
can support you with
prayers and confidence as
you stay or leave.
```

The early days of September 1944 became more action-packed and tension-filled. The march of refugees was increasing. The city itself was badly wrecked by the continuing bombings. A large number of people were joining the stream of people moving west. Now the hospital was ministering to soldiers. They came every day. By September 10, even the soldiers stopped. They were not coming to Wuzhou. They were coming through Wuzhou. It did not take a military strategist to know that the Chinese army was defeated.

Still Bill waited. His staff continued to trust his judgment. He could not leave with a hospital full of patients. Hoping to reduce the number of patients in the hospital, he and his staff began to treat patients and move them out as soon as possible. By September 12, they were able to evacuate all but a few of the more seriously wounded. On September 12, Bill received word that the city itself would be evacuated. Now he made his decision. It was time to go. If they stayed, their task might be ended forever. If they left and followed the people west, they could continue their ministry to sick people. On the night of September 12, 1944, Bill called his staff together and outlined his plan.

They would take every possible piece of equipment with them and load the barges. They would go west until they found a place that was safe. There they would find some kind of quarters to set up their hospital. They would continue to serve. The Stout Memorial Hospital would not die. It would move, but it would not die. The hospital was not the building any more than a church is a building. The hospital was the staff, and the spirit of service was in the name of the Lord Jesus Christ. They would move the hospital.

All of this Bill said simply, but the dream the missionary doctor envisioned thrilled his staff. They enthusiastically prepared for the move. It took four days to dismantle the equipment and load the barges. They worked mostly at night because Japanese fighter planes were a constant threat. Bill turned over the medical chores to his capable residents and supervised the move. His fellow workers marveled at his ability. He dismantled complicated machines and reduced bulky items to compact kits. These could be crated and loaded onto the large barges the governor had stationed at the Wuzhou docks three months before.

On the night of September 16, a final check was made at the hospital. Then the staff walked through the deserted streets, carrying what few belongings they were taking for themselves. There were brief backward looks at the proud hospital building, battle-scarred, but still standing. The building symbolized all they were doing. It had come to mean to them what it meant to the people, "the life of China."

As Bill walked through the streets of Wuzhou, he noticed the havoc. Small fires were still burning from the day's raid. They cast an eerie glow on the shadowy staff. At Bill's insistence, white uniforms had been packed. The staff was dressed in the black muslin that was summer dress for most Chinese. They would be easy enough targets on the river without their white clothing.

Bill and his staff boarded the barges. The

small gunboat that would pull them to safety strained against the towlines. Slowly, the barge moved out into the broad West River beneath the peaceful September moon. Their journey into the wilderness had begun.

Chapter 28: Hospital on the Move

Dawn the next day found the group well upriver from Wuzhou. They took cover at the edge of the river under sheltering bamboos. The next night's journey brought them to the mouth of a small river, which led to a relatively obscure town, Yung-Yuen. Because Yung-Yuen was in such an out-of-the-way place, Bill thought it would be a safer place to go. The town was bound to be filled with refugees. The main Japanese drives were aimed at larger cities. Not knowing how long they would be safe on the river, Bill ordered the motor launch to pull into the tributary and head for Yung-Yuen.

Their progress up the river was little more than a painful creep. The current was much stronger than they thought. On the second day, Japanese planes roared overhead. All the people had to abandon the barges and take cover in caves along the river's edge.

That evening Bill was supervising the

reloading of a barge when he heard someone call, "Waa I Saang! Waa I Saang! Come here at once!"

He saw Dr. Wong calling him from a point up the trail near the river. Standing by him was a Chinese peasant loaded down with his few possessions.

"What is the matter, Dr. Wong?" Bill asked as he came near them.

"This man has just come from Yung-Yuen. He says the Japanese have taken the town and are moving down this river toward Tun Yuen. He says they cannot be more than ten miles behind him."

"It is God's will we stopped in these caves," Bill said. "Now let's get going."

He ran down to the motor launch. In a few moments the loading was complete. They turned back toward Tun Yuen and the West River.

The group made much faster progress travelling with the current of the river, but Bill had a new worry. Not only were the Japanese just ten miles behind them, but he was afraid they might also be directly ahead. Earlier in the day he heard on his radio that Wuzhou had fallen. No date was given. He did not know how long after their departure the Japanese had arrived, but he knew the drive was moving toward them. Japanese gunboats might be ahead of them. But, he thought, looking into the darkness ahead, 'There is no other place to go.' They would not stand a chance if they tried to take to the hills. Praying silently, he waited for the dawn.

Shortly after dawn they arrived at Tun Yuen. They had made the return journey in a third of the time it had taken them to move upriver. To their great relief, the Japanese had not arrived.

Again, they pulled out into the broad West River and continued a westerly course. The next town was Kwei Peng, where again they faced a choice. They could go north toward Leizhou, a strong military point which the Chinese and Americans together might hold. To the west was Nanning.

Calling his doctors together, Bill spread out the map and outlined the possibilities. If they went to Leizhou, they would be able to go only so far by boat. Then they would have to find some kind of land transportation. It would be much cheaper to go by river to Nanning. However, the Japanese drive from Indochina was moving in that direction. They had no way of knowing how much progress they were making. But, as one of the doctors pointed out, they also did not know how close the Japanese were to Leizhou. Bill made his decision. They would go to Nanning. At least it would allow them to stay with their barges and prevent the delay of unloading them or the tragedy of abandoning their equipment.

Still another problem confronted him. West from Kwei Peng the gunboat pulling the barges would be used for battle. It could not go with them any farther. Taking a doctor with him who knew Mandarin, Bill went into Kwei Peng to find the owners of the few launches in town. They looked to hire someone to take them to Nanning. He found someone, after agreeing to pay a lot of money for the service.

Food was more and more difficult to find. Except for the supplies they brought with them, Bill and his group depended on small amounts of rice purchased at very high prices.

The next few days were a long nightmare. First they came to rapids which the launch could not navigate. Bill organized his already weakened staff into crews to pull heavy towlines to clear the rapids. They worked for hours at the exhausting task. Finally, when all of them were once again on the barges, over half the staff had diarrhea and fever.

Like a watchful father, Bill made the rounds of patients on each barge, giving them medicines and offering encouragement. When he could do no more, he threw down his mat in their midst and collapsed for a few hours of sleep.

The Chinese had been accustomed to foreigners, even missionaries, having separate quarters and eating different food. This was normal and even expected of "white" people. But Bill Wallace, the revered Waa I Saang, slept among them, accepted the portions and food they ate, and even turned aside food himself so they might have it. One of them said, "He actually lived before us the life of Christ."

The strange caravan was met by military authorities in Nanning, and Bill was told it would not be safe to stay there. They advised him to proceed to the little town of Poseh. The authorities felt the Japanese would be contained at Nanning. If Bill and his group could reach Poseh, they should be able to stop and begin their ministry.

But Bill's expensive transportation was gone. He was left with the clumsy, heavily loaded barges and no power to move on. Working through the day, Bill and the men of his staff summoned all their skills and rigged up clumsy but fairly effective sails for each barge. Then, with towlines and long poles, they moved toward Poseh. When they were fortunate, the wind furnished enough power to keep them inching along. At other times, they used poles to move through the shallow water near the bank of the river. At still other times, they poled, pulled, and tried to sail in order to keep ahead of the Japanese behind them.

Nearly night of the first day out of Nanning, Bill sat down on a box at the rear of the last barge. He wanted to send a note to Dr. Rankin to let him know they had escaped. Bill had forgotten how many days they had been out, but he knew that friends and families would be worried. In his broad handwriting, he wrote,

> We left Wuzhou on September 16 just ahead of the Japanese. 'We' includes our hospital equipment and staff and nurses, a total of fifty-five people. We had actually hoped to reestablish ourselves in Nanning, but we were told to move to Poseh in southern Guangxi. It will probably take us ten days to

get there if we get there at all.

Moving expenses have been tremendous and now we are facing a hard winter, but we are doing our best to keep the Stout Memorial Hospital intact. It's the hope of every one of us that it not die. Our staff and nurses have been faithful to the hospital through it all. It is our wish that someday, some happy day, we may return to Wuzhou. I do not know if we can survive or not, but we're going to try. And if we fail, we will have the assurance that we failed trying.

Be good. BILL WALLACE.

As he finished the letter, he was aware that Dr. Wong was beside him. Together they watched the twilight give way to night. Since leaving Nanning, they had marked its location by a great pillar of smoke. The Japanese scorched earth policy meant everything in the city was burning. Now as night fell, the pillar of smoke glowed red with the fires that fed it.

The Chinese Christian said, "We are like the people of Israel in the wilderness. We have a pillar of cloud by day and a pillar of fire by night."

Chapter 29: Lucy Wright Arrives

The American transport plane banked sharply and began to descend through the thick clouds shielding its destination. Lucy Wright pressed her face against the window for the first glimpse of Poseh. She was sure the pilot had miscalculated and would fly right into the ground when the plane broke through the clouds. The south China countryside greeted her with deep greens and rich browns. Directly ahead was a gray huddle of buildings and the Poseh airstrip. She desperately hoped she would find the refugee staff of the Stout Memorial Hospital.

She thanked the crew-cut Georgia boy who had flown her from the village where she had been waiting out the Japanese offensive. Then she picked up her duffel bag and walked quickly toward a Quonset hut she assumed was the terminal. There, she learned that a Chinese hospital group headed by an American missionary had already left.

"They stayed here a week," an American soldier told her. "Dr. Wallace operated a combined Chinese-American hospital, serving both the military and the citizens."

Lucy asked, "Did they go back to Nanning?"

"Yes," the soldier replied. "Dr. Wallace said it was time to begin to push back toward Wuzhou. He thought victory was on its way. That's one of the hardest-working outfits I've ever seen," he added seriously. "And he helped me through a rough sickness."

The soldier told Lucy how Bill had tenderly treated him for a case of hookworm. He also told her he was a Baptist from Dallas, Texas.

"Somehow, I've got to catch up with Dr. Wallace and his hospital group," Lucy said.

"You might hitch a ride with those trucks at the other end of the field, if you're lucky. They are going to Nanning, I hear," the soldier said.

Moments later, Lucy was in the cab of a truck loaded with relief supplies. She was on her way to Nanning.

"Have you been to Nanning?" she asked the driver.

"Yes, ma'am. I'm stationed there. But if you haven't been there, I wouldn't want you to get your hopes up. It's not much town."

"Never mind that. Do you know where Dr. Wallace is located?"

"Dr. Wallace? I'm afraid not, ma'am. Nanning is crawling with people from all over China."

"Guess you would not have a chance to see him, at that." Lucy was disappointed. She was afraid they had moved again. She was ready to give up of ever reaching the group she had set out to help in the fall 1943. It was now June 1945.

"Wait a minute," the driver said. "Are you talking about a tall, thin American? A missionary with about fifty Chinese with him?"

"That's right. That's Bill Wallace," Lucy said.

"I can take you right by there. I didn't know his name, but everybody knows about him. That crowd is a legend in these parts. I hear they came from 'way down the West River.' They sailed right through the entire Japanese army. The Chinese think they're protected by angels or something."

"They're from Wuzhou," Lucy volunteered. "I have been trying to catch up with them for over a year."

"Well, hold on, ma'am. You're practically there!"

Moments later, Lucy, wearing dust-covered army fatigues, hurried to find Bill. When she identified herself, she touched off a big celebration! Bill was so excited he made a 45-minute speech! Lucy, who spoke Mandarin, couldn't understand Bill's Tennessee-accented Cantonese. But she sensed what he was saying from the faces of his hearers. As Bill talked in slow, now measured, now faltering words, Lucy realized the little band had become a close-knit Christian family by the hardships they had endured together. She felt the same pride in joining them that she thought soldiers must feel when they become part of a proud and honored military unit. She found herself envying them and the experiences that had brought them together.

"And we will return soon." She could tell he was talking of the future now and leading them with him. "We will return to Wuzhou. We will rebuild, and this old hospital will keep right on with an unbroken history. I believe God has spared us for this task."

It was not an eloquent speech, but Lucy wished she could take it down word for word. She was sure that Bill's heart was more open in this moment than ever before.

Days later she heard the story of their adventures from one of the English-speaking nurses with whom she was rooming. She had known of their trek to Poseh, but from there she had only pieces of the story.

"Where in the world did you stay in Poseh?" Lucy asked. "I was there this morning, and it doesn't look like much."

"It wasn't much," the Chinese nurse answered. "Dr. Wallace went to the authorities. He told them we were a hospital group and would like to set up and serve the people there. The town elders said we could use an old Confucian temple and an abandoned school building. Actually, it was Governor Wong of Guangxi who made this possible, the same man who made the boat available for us. We were overwhelmed by this generous act until we realized they let us have the temple because no one else would use it. The townspeople said it was inhabited by devils. After we moved in, we became local heroes because the people figured Dr. Wallace purged the place of the demons who were possessing it."

Lucy laughed, "The medical association would appreciate Dr. Wallace's abilities to cast out demons."

"Well, I don't know about that, but under his leadership, we soon transformed that filthy place into a hospital. You've never seen so many makeshift odds and ends in your life. Dr. Wallace brought in electric power. He set up a water and sewage system. He helped us set up bamboo curtains and find mats to use as beds. He even managed to find a chemical that he mixed to restore our uniforms to their original whiteness. He always wanted us looking and acting like a hospital."

Lucy was silent. The nurse continued, "Poseh had lots of cases of malaria. Also, cholera and other diseases were rampant. It seemed three quarters of the population was sick. We were no exception. Nearly half our staff was sick with malaria. We were also easy prey for other diseases because we were weak from poor food and the stress of our trip. One of the nurses developed a severe malaria psychosis. Have you ever seen one of those?"

Lucy nodded. She remembered the horror of patients screaming in the night, totally out of their minds with the ravages of the fever.

"You should have seen Dr. Wallace with her. She was like an animal, and it was as if he had some kind of magic charm. When nobody else was able to do anything with her, he quieted her. He stayed by her bedside for forty-eight hours until he was sure she was through the crisis.

"Up to this time, we had lost no one. I am sorry to say that ended at Poseh. You see, we heard that the Japanese were threatening Poseh. We thought we were safe. Then, American planes spotted a column of Japanese who had bypassed Nanning. They were only twenty miles from us. We were heartsick. We were so tired, we were ready to stay there and take whatever came. Dr. Wallace got us to our feet again. Somehow we repacked our equipment. As we were trying to figure out how to get it back to the boats, he drove up with an ambulance he had found someplace. To this day, I don't know where he got it.

"When the ambulance was about to complete hauling our equipment to the boats, we discovered one of our doctors, Dr. Chow Kwan Pok, was very sick. Dr. Wallace was treating him for ulcers, but without the proper diet, he suffered a severe relapse. He began bleeding internally right at the time we should have been leaving. We could hear guns in the distance.

"Dr. Wallace would not hear of moving him. We sat there while he did everything he could for Dr. Pok, but in that place there was so little we could do. I'll never forget that night. We were not allowed to have any light because the Japanese planes had bombed Poseh several times. Silently, we sat around the building watching Dr. Wallace bend over his patient.

Not many of us slept that night. The guns were coming closer and closer. Just before dawn, Dr. Wallace urged us all to get on the boat and go, but then it was our turn to be insistent. We refused, but I think he was grateful for it.

"Dr. Pok died shortly after dawn. Dr. Wallace had done all he could do. I never want to be in a situation like that again. We were actually praying that he would either recover enough to travel or go ahead and die. I know it sounds terrible, but you cannot imagine how scary it was hearing those guns coming closer and knowing Dr. Pok's life was hanging in the balance."

Lucy could imagine the drama of the moment, but she knew that was nothing compared to the actual experience.

"This was the only time I came close to getting impatient with Waa I Saang. He was adamant about securing a coffin and giving Dr. Pok a Christian burial. All the stores were closed and barred. Most of the townspeople had fled. Dr. Wallace and the evangelist finally located a funeral-shop owner who had not left. Waa I Saang bought a coffin from him, but the man would not help him transport it back to where we were. Dr. Wallace had to take it apart, and we carried it piece by piece to a small hill back of the old temple. There Dr. Wallace put the coffin back together and then he carried the body of Dr. Pok up the hill, where we held the funeral.

"Now the guns, nearer than ever, were being rivaled by thunder from the heavens. Just before we began the service, it started to rain. Someone said, 'Heaven cries with us on this day.' Dr. Wallace read some Scripture passages from his little pocket New Testament and led a prayer. Then each of us picked up some of the dirt which was now almost mud and tossed it in. As soon as the grave was filled, we ran down the hill to the river and boarded the boats."

The nurse's cheeks were wet now. She paused and dabbed her face with a small handkerchief.

"That may have been our saddest moment, but it certainly wasn't our most difficult. Poling and pulling the boats, we moved on down to a little village called Fok-Luk. The conditions there were horrible. Refugees were everywhere. Bodies were lying in the streets. There was no one to move them. We had to avoid wild pigs who were eating the dead. The pigs were so hungry they sometimes attacked the living. People were too weak even to catch them.

"A Japanese army had moved up from Indochina to the south and was trying to join the army that had taken Nanning. We were trapped in the middle. We camped outside Fok-Luk and daily ran to the nearby caves to take refuge from the Japanese dive bombers. Those caves were sweltering masses of stinking flesh. I still remember their stench. And the fear. You could smell the fear.

"This was the time I think we were in most danger. Many of us were ready to move off on our own and find food where we could, but Dr. Wallace kept us together. He encouraged us, led us in prayer, rationed the food, and went out daily to find more.

"It was while at Fok-Luk that I saw Dr. Wallace refuse his rice allowance and give it to a nurse who was very sick with fever. Most of us were sick with diarrhea or fever. Later on, I saw him behind the cook tent we had rigged up. He was eating grains of burned rice, hardly worth eating, that had been thrown away. When he realized I had seen him, he was terribly embarrassed.

"He wasn't ashamed of eating that food. No one else would have had it, as hungry as we were. I think he was embarrassed because he did not want me to know how hungry he was.

"He was so thin I thought he would blow away if a good wind came along. Somehow, however, he stayed well. He showed us how to eat the bones of what few birds we found. He said we needed to eat them for the vitamins. I believe his methods saved all our lives. He was so good, watching over each of us, cheering us, caring for the sick, and doing everything he could to provide for our comfort.

"I don't want to offend you, Miss Wright, but we Chinese are not used to seeing Americans or Europeans do things like this. We know the missionaries love us, but there was always a difference. They lived their way and we lived ours, but Dr. Wallace didn't know about the difference. He was one of us. He accepted our portion, all of it."

"I can see why you all love him as you do," Lucy said. "How long were you there before you returned to Poseh?"

"I am afraid we weren't thinking about returning then. The Japanese killed several soldiers right outside Fok-Luk about a week after we arrived. We fled for our lives during the night. We left our equipment where it was. Fortunately, we were able to recover it later.

"This time we moved by foot to a little village called Tung-Ling. This was the time I felt most sorry for Dr. Wallace. In pulling the boat along the banks of the river out of Nanning, he had worn out his one pair of shoes, a ragged pair of tennis shoes. Now he was walking through the paper he had stuffed in the bottom of them.

"He fell down by the side of the road the second day. We were all afraid he'd had a heart attack or something. An American soldier had given us two horses the day before. We put him up on one and kept going. When he recovered enough to realize what was happening, he insisted on getting off and putting one of the nurses on. I don't know how we lived during those days. We just existed at Tung-Ling. It was a wonderful day when a column of American soldiers came through and told us that Poseh had been retaken."

"And you were all still together?" Lucy asked.

"All together." The nurse smiled. "And you have never seen a more grateful group. Daily we prayed. Our prayers were loud, and our tears were many, but daily we sought God.

"That was the only time we broke up for a while. Dr. Wallace found transportation for us a few at a time with American trucks that were coming through. The soldiers seemed so surprised to see him way out there. It cheered us to watch him laughing and talking with people from back home.

"When we all got back to Poseh, he came in a few days later with our equipment. That's when we began our hospital. I think the hospital was Dr. Wallace's idea. We joined together with the other medical people, including the military, and established the Chinese-American Combined Hospital."

Lucy said, "You must have been treating a lot of American soldiers. I met one back in Poseh who had been in your hospital with hookworm."

"Yes, we treated people with ulcers, and soldiers infected with hookworm, dysentery, nutritional diarrhea, malaria, relapsing fever, all of it. After one particularly hard battle with a pocket of Japanese nearby, we treated the wounded. But we also lost one of our nurses at that time. We never knew exactly what she died of, but it was like losing a sister. Dr. Wallace mourned her as a daughter."

Nurse Luk stopped and smiled. "And by God's grace, we've been here ever since."

"Yes," Lucy said, "by God's grace."

The next day, after Bill introduced her to the hospital routine, Lucy made calls with him. She was amazed at how well he got along with both the Chinese and American soldiers being treated there. She noticed he had a unique sense of humor and the ability to get people to talk about themselves and their interests. It was an effective form of therapy.

The hospital was a 150-bed unit, if you can call strung rope and straw mats hospital beds. Late that day, however, as she assisted him in surgery, she realized that this hospital had nothing to be sorry for, even in such primitive conditions.

The hospital in the wilderness served through the summer in Nanning. On August 14, 1945, now known as V-J Day, the Japanese emperor surrendered unconditionally. His armies were leaving China.

The hospital group could hardly believe it. They were going home! All day long the hospital became the scene for celebrations. Lucy saw grateful American soldiers come bringing food and other gifts. The crisp discipline of the wards dissolved into joy. The center of attention, despite all his effort to fade into the background, was the grinning doctor who had faithfully fulfilled the role of Moses during these days in the wilderness.

The next day the military staged a formal celebration and the Stout Memorial nurses were asked to sing. Their voices rang out with joy and gratitude. That evening, at a party sponsored by the Americans, they were asked to sing again. Like many celebrations in those days, the party had become extremely wild, with a lot of drinking. Lucy and the other nurses were used to singing hymns. They didn't know what to do. They turned to Bill, seeking advice. He grinned and said, "Get up there and sing a hymn." They did, and the people loved it!

Their hymn touched the hearts of the better side of those celebrating. It turned

their thoughts from unrestrained drinking to
memories of home, to the faith of their fathers,
and to their gratitude to an almighty God.
It was a fitting climax to the ministry of the
hospital in the wilderness.

The same God who provided for them to
leave Wuzhou now provided for their return.
Grateful American officials, many who had
experienced the ministry of the "refugeeing
hospital" firsthand, threw themselves
enthusiastically into the project of returning
the hospital staff. A large flatboat was found
for a ridiculously low price. Bill wondered
what had taken place to get such a good deal.
Shortly, a motor launch was provided to tow
them. Then, American soldiers attached to
the units Dr. Wallace and his staff had served,
built a kitchen boat that could be towed along
behind the barge. It would carry the staff and
its equipment.

On a sparkling September morning, they
began the last leg of their journey. The docks of
Nanning were lined with grateful citizens and
cheering soldiers. As the staff waved to their
friends, the broad West River moved them
along. Soon Nanning faded into the distance.
They were on their way home.

It was a four-day trip, but very different
from the painful flight they had taken nearly a
year earlier. It was a time of rest and singing
and individual meditation. Lucy noticed that
Bill sat on the sidelines most of the journey,
aware of the exhaustion that comes from a total
experience.

All afternoon of the last day of the trip,

the staff laughed and called out to one another as familiar scenes appeared on the horizon.

As they gathered for their evening meal, they decided to sing hymns into Wuzhou. Then the lights of Wuzhou came into view. They saw the familiar skyline and hills. Rising to their feet, they sang together,

> Crown Him with many crowns,
> The Lamb upon His throne;
> Hark! how the heavenly anthem drowns
> All music but its own:
>
> Awake, my soul, and sing
> Of Him who died for thee;
> And hail Him as thy matchless King
> Through all eternity.

Lucy Wright looked up as the smiling doctor approached with a letter in his hand. He said, "I have just written my sister, and I thought you might like to read the letter."

She took it and read it by firelight. Never had so much been said with so little.

> DEAR Sis:
> Wuzhou. Love,
> BILL

Chapter 30: Home at Wuzhou

The hospital building still stood strong, but the interior and grounds were in shambles. The terrible destruction, along with the cholera that was making many people in Wuzhou very sick, depressed the returning staff. Only the wide grins of the welcoming people cheered them.

Bill led his fellow physicians on a survey of the hospital. The plumbing was clogged with brick and filth. The Japanese soldiers had stabled horses on the lower floor. There was no water, power, screens, or doors. The furniture was destroyed or gone. Vital pieces of hard-to-replace equipment were strewn over the grounds. A section of the roof was gone.

After the survey, Bill gathered the staff together at the steps. They looked tattered and tired. Their faces showed the almost impossible task they faced. Bill stood quietly looking over the group for a moment and then grinned. "We had better get with it. There are some sick people around here, and they need a hospital."

With that he turned and started up the steps. One by one they followed him. Shortly, they were working together happily to reclaim the old building. There was a job to be done.

They cleaned equipment. They screened, scrubbed, and painted the first floor. It was reasonably clean within a matter of days. Bill rigged up a way to make saline that could treat the cholera. He set up a crude but effective laboratory. With a borrowed torch, he converted some Japanese gasoline drums into a large storage tank for the water they boiled day and night. Using the mechanical skills he learned as a teenager, he built a hand-powered electric generator to provide power and light for surgery. At one point, he even cleared the building and defused three unexploded Japanese bombs!

Daily, he encouraged his staff to work hard to receive their first patient as soon as possible. The staff responded by working to their limits. Just one week later, a proud and grateful group of doctors and nurses gathered in the bomb-scarred fifth-floor chapel to dedicate themselves to the task. Then they went downstairs and threw open the wrought iron gates. The Stout Memorial Hospital was open again!

Bill carried very little medical responsibility for the first few weeks. He worked instead on rebuilding the hospital. He rebuilt the kitchen, personally constructing the brick oven they were to use for over a year.

Since no construction men were available, he hired laborers and supervised the repair of the roof section that had been blasted away. This was his first failure; it fell in a week. Surveying the wreckage, he said, "Well, you can't win them all," and started over.

The staff were concerned about Bill's constant work with never a moment to relax. Lucy accused Bill of not taking enough care of himself.

"I'll declare," she said, "he takes absolutely no thought for himself. He sleeps on a bamboo mat with a smooth log for a pillow. We found two or three old beds, but he gave me one and sent the others to the nurses' quarters. He said he had been a refugee so long he couldn't sleep on a bed.

"One day I managed to buy some buffalo milk, oatmeal, and Indian butter and prepared him a meal. The way he carried on, you would have thought it was an embassy dinner.

"He has a childlike enthusiasm for the little things in life, and it is catching. One night he hollered for us to come to the door. We came running, expecting some kind of emergency. Instead, he wanted us to see our first full moon since returning to Wuzhou."

Two months after their return, Bill heard of an outbreak of typhoid fever in the Wuzhou jail. It was a pitiful place, crowded with political prisoners and common criminals. He went to the city fathers and told them it was a health menace to the whole city. They gave permission for his staff to stamp out the typhus.

Daily, he took volunteers to the prison and made the rounds of the dirty cells and the sick inmates. Even the most distrustful and hardened prisoners saw him as an angel of mercy. He threatened and even bribed those in charge to make some much needed improvements. He surprised those who knew him with his passion about the project.

By Christmas Bill had the hospital back on a teaching level with a new class of nurses and two new interns. Returning from a trip to a nearby village one day, he set down a sack of bleached bones, the remains of a poor peasant who had died from unknown causes along the trail. Soon he had a perfect skeleton and instructed his nurses in basic bone structure.

The next spring, he received the glad news that Dr. Robert Beddoe was on his way back to China and the Stout Memorial Hospital. As soon as he arrived, Bill would take his second trip to the U.S. He was very excited! He needed some more study, and, of course, he wanted to see his sister and her family.

Then the Beddoes arrived. After a short reunion, Bill was gone, Knoxville bound.

Chapter 31: In the States Again

Bill had planned this time in the U.S. to better prepare himself to practice "the best medicine." Great strides had been made in surgical and medical techniques during the war years. Bill wanted to master what he could before returning to China. It was a time to "sharpen his tools." As he had often lectured the resident physicians who worked beside him in China, "The physician's education is an ever-continuing one. A doctor cannot rest on his laurels."

His first tour was at Chicago's famous Cook County School of Medicine. He enrolled in three courses. From October to January, he worked in the medical center. Bill was excited to learn new techniques. He also spent a lot of time at the medical library, reading medical journals to learn about breakthroughs in research. He loved to watch surgeries, and he asked many questions of many well-known surgeons.

When he finished his courses in Chicago, he made a brief trip to Knoxville to visit his sister and her family. Then he went to New Orleans to study tropical medicines at Tulane University.

From a career standpoint, Bill should have studied surgery. Instead, he chose to work in an area that would better equip him to serve the Chinese.

In his rare moments of free time in New Orleans, Bill attended lectures at a nearby cancer clinic. In China he had noticed many cases of skin cancer among people of a particular area served by Stout Memorial Hospital. He made many notes and observations so he could pass the information on to his medical staff and other doctors in Wuzhou.

When spring came, he thought again about returning to China. Dr. Beddoe wrote that he was urgently needed. Dr. Beddoe was about to retire, and he knew he could not do the work at Stout much longer. The people were ready for Waa I Saang to return.

In April, Dr. Rankin visited Bill at New Orleans and later wrote Beddoe:

```
Bill seems to have just
one single idea in mind:
to get back to Wuzhou as
soon as possible.
```

Bill was excited about the prospects for his work. Dr. Rankin had brought wonderful news. Another doctor was being appointed and would sail soon for language school. Also, an experienced nurse had been appointed to serve at Wuzhou. A dedicated young evangelist and his family were already in language school, and they would also be sent to Wuzhou. Bill's hopes soared.

Early in May, Bill completed his work in New Orleans and returned to Knoxville. In Knoxville, he completed his plans to return to China. Two days before he was to leave for San Francisco, he received a call from Dr. Herbert Acuff, a lifelong friend.

"William, I have some good news for you. You have been elected as a fellow in the International College of Surgeons."

Bill was stunned. He was aware that Dr. Peters had kept a file on some of his more interesting cases in China. Earlier in the year he had also given his old friend a full account of his medical findings during his twelve years in China. He did not know why the doctor was so interested in having the records, photos, and other papers. The International College of Surgeons! He thought he gave that up the day he turned down Dr. Peters' offer to join him.

"I don't know what to say, Dr. Acuff. I would not have thought that I qualified."

"You qualify, William. Perhaps in a way few others have. You have done surgery of a nature and on a scale that makes many of us seem inexperienced by comparison. You deserve it, and I'm honored to be the one to inform you."

Bill had given up the thought of fame and prestige to plant his life in China. But his light was too bright to ignore. His profession had recognized him and was proud of him. It made him all the more eager to return to the work God had called him to do. It was hard to feel noble, he decided, when you were so busy feeling grateful. His colleagues in Wuzhou discovered his honor quite by accident. Bill never mentioned it.

Finally, the day came for Bill to leave Knoxville. The Stegalls tried their best to be cheerful as they drove Bill to the airport in Knoxville. He had gained twenty-two pounds during the year and looked very healthy. In fact, his sister decided he never looked better. But that did not relieve the sadness she felt when it came time to say goodbye. Bill sensed it, but he was so intent on returning to his work he did not respond.

Sydney Stegall said, "Take care of yourself, William, and drop us a line from time to time." Bill's brother-in-law, a Knoxville businessman, managed Bill's records and bought things Bill needed for the hospital in China. He considered it part of his Christian responsibility, and he loved Bill like his own brother.

"Even if it's only an order for a set of test tubes, it lets us know you are OK."

Bill looked at Sydney and then at his sister, Ruth Lynn, and their son, Sandy. Sandy was trying hard not to cry.

"Chief, I don't have a worry in the world. You will take care of Sis and Sandy, and I'll take care of me. The Lord will watch over us all."

Chapter 32: Bill's Third Term Begins

Despite the uncertainties in China, Bill was excited to begin a third term as a missionary there. Dr. Sam Rankin and his wife, Miriam, were in language school in Guangzhou. Nurse Everley Hayes, Ed Galloway and his family were there, too. In less than a year they would be working in Wuzhou.

The promise of new faces reminded Bill of the others who had gone to work in other areas. Rex Ray was now working at a leper colony, and Bill missed him. The Beddoes retired soon after Bill returned to China. Bill did not realize until they were gone how much he loved Dr. Beddoe, who was so different from him. The hospital was now officially Bill's responsibility. Always before it had been a temporary assignment. He felt the burden, but the hospital was prospering. His 1947 report was short but deep.

        Every effort has been made

> to fulfill the mission of
> this hospital. The blind
> receive their sight and
> the halt and lame walk.
> The lepers are cleansed.
> The deaf hear, and the
> poor have the gospel
> preached to them. It
> is our hope and prayer
> that the medical service
> offered here will honor
> the gospel we preach each
> day.

Another face was there only briefly. Lucy Wright, who served so well during the rebuilding, was near death when Bill returned from the U.S. Lucy needed surgery, but neither Dr. Beddoe nor the Chinese surgeons felt they had the skills to do it. Bill took over when he returned.

An operation did seem necessary, but it was extremely dangerous. Bill wanted to be sure it was the only chance Lucy had. He decided to wait out her progress with fluids and medicines. Again and again he whispered, "You are going to make it, Lucy. Stay in there. You are going to lick it."

Then he prayed. Several times he called others to join him to pray at Lucy's bedside. Bill believed deeply in the power of prayer. He often read and quoted James 5:14-15 to his resident doctors and nurses: "Is anyone among you sick? He should call for the elders of the church, and they should pray over him after anointing him with olive oil in the name of the Lord. The prayer of faith will save the sick person, and the Lord will restore him to health; if he has committed sins, he will be forgiven."

Bill counted medical skills and drugs as resources from God, but they were never the only resource. Too many people who were facing death had gotten well with no medical explanation. He knew that God alone had the power to make people well.

As Bill and others prayed, Lucy, without surgery, began to get better. Bill appeared in her room one day with a heavy medical book. He opened it, showed her a marked section and then said, "God's done his part. Let's do ours. Here is your problem." Then he turned the page. "Here is your cure."

Laying the volume on her nightstand, he stood up and smiled. "Now, don't dawdle."

Lucy recovered, but time in the U.S. and a long recovery were ahead. She left for the States after a tearful farewell. Only Jessie Green remained of the prewar missionary staff with whom Bill had served.

Bill thought about the changing scene. It hardly seemed possible that he was now "the oldest" Baptist missionary in Wuzhou. And yet, he knew he, too, had changed. He was older, and his hair was thinner. But his hand was steady, and he was surer of himself. He was grateful for the experiences of the past, and he was grateful for the opportunities of the present. If the calm of these days turned out to be temporary, he was still ready to work while it was day.

Chapter 33: Bill Gets Sick

In the summer of 1948, Wuzhou was hit by an epidemic of paratyphoid. Bill ordered each staff member to be vaccinated and later went to get serum to protect himself. The serum was a new typhoid-paratyphoid combination. It was stored alongside the older typhoid serum which it replaced. Somehow Bill got the older serum. Later he became very sick with paratyphoid.

The Chinese doctors worked over him desperately. At first, he was able to direct the treatment, then gradually he became delirious. He was a boy again, sick with typhoid. He could make out the features of his father hovering over him, tenderly caring for him. He cried out, "Paps, I'm burning up!"

Nurse Luk wiped his brow and tried to calm him. At times, he was rational.

"Get Newbern," he said. He lifted himself up on one arm. Again he gasped, "Tell Newbern I must see him."

William Newbern was Bill's friend from

the Christian and Missionary Alliance group.
They had spent many hours together. When he
heard of Bill's illness, he rushed to be with him.

Reaching up, Bill pulled him closer.

"Tell the others to leave. I must make a
confession."

Newbern gripped the clutching fingers
of his friend. "I'm going to stay right here, Bill.
You are going to be all right."

"Please," Bill's voice was weak, but
urgent, "please, Newbern, hear my confession."

Tears glistened on the preacher's cheeks.
Who was he to hear this man's confession? It
would be better if he confessed to Bill, fever
and all. But at Bill's insistence, he sent the
others out. When he returned, Bill had lapsed
back into his delirium. Patiently, Newbern
waited. In a moment, the suffering doctor
opened his eyes again.

"I've wronged my Lord, Newbern.
I've neglected him terribly." Falling back, he
groaned in agony while his friend listened
quietly.

"I've been more concerned with the
material prosperity of the hospital than I have
with knowing my Lord. I've been too busy for
him." He tried to rise. "Pray for me, Newbern.
Pray for me."

William Newbern was so choked up he
could hardly speak. Bill's faith was so simple
and uncomplicated. But he prayed.

In a moment, Bill gasped, "God is
sufficient." He could trust his Lord. However,
the disease continued, and he grew steadily
weaker.

The next day brought light into the room again, but not hope. Bill's fever-wracked body twisted. His dry, cracked lips couldn't make words. Dr. Wong Taai Ning, Bill's doctor, was very worried. He made quick notes on the chart. Then, stretching, he walked to the window. It had been a long night. Cushioning his head against his arm, Dr. Ning looked out over the city of Wuzhou to the West River. The morning fog rested on the surface of the water. He turned to look again at Bill.

Movement below the window drew his attention to a silent, waiting crowd. Had they been there all night? It was a strange mix of people from all over the city. As he watched, Nurse Luk walked from the building and began talking to someone among the waiting people. She gestured, shaking her head slowly. The low moan that moved among the people reminded Wong how very much his people loved Bill.

He turned as the door opened. He greeted Dr. Leung, a resident surgeon.

"How is Waa I Saang?"

"He is weak."

"Ai, the fever has made him thin."

"Yes. He is very thin, but he was never with much flesh."

"No, he ran up and down the stairs continually. He always worked too hard." They were silent.

"Is there nothing else we can do?"

"Paratyphoid is especially hard on foreigners. His pulse is weaker. I really fear for him."

"Ai."

Dr. Wong became aware that someone had joined them. He turned and greeted Miss Jessie Green. Afraid to look at Bill, she looked to Dr. Ning for an encouraging word. Helpless, he simply looked back to the thin features of the missionary surgeon.

With sudden determination, Jessie Green said, "I am going to wire the new doctors at Guangzhou. Would you mind?"

"Oh, no, Miss Neung. But I fear, even if they come it will be only to share our grief."

"Nevertheless, I will wire them."

She hurried down the stairs and worked her way through the crowd at the door. A girl tugged at her sleeve. The little face looked up at her. The scar of an operation for harelip was barely visible.

"Will Waa I Saang die?"

"We hope not, little one. You pray to the Lord Jesus to make him well."

"Yes, Miss Neung, I will do that."

Jessie Green's telegram reached Sam Rankin during the South China Mission meeting. It was hard for him to think of Bill near death. For several years he had heard of the magnificent ministry of the modest Tennessean. He looked forward to working by his side, to catch his spirit, and to learn from his surgical skill.

By afternoon, he was on the West River steamer for Wuzhou. The next day he stood anxiously on the boat as Wuzhou came into sight. Beside him stood Dr. Don Moore, who had volunteered to come with him, and Nurse Everley Hayes. Impatiently, they watched the muddy waters churn as the West River steamer maneuvered alongside the Wuzhou landing. Then Rankin spied Jessie Green on the dock.

"Here, Jessie! How is Bill?"

Her look gave him a moment of panic. Were they too late?

"Thank God, you are here. There has been no change, but please come now. This boy will bring your things."

In the highly musical tones of Cantonese, she gave directions to the boy. Then she turned and led them through the crowded streets toward the hospital compound.

By the following day the doctors had done all they could do. There was really very little anyone could do. Perhaps the liquids slowly dripping into his veins would make up for the dehydration, but would they help in time? Everly Hayes had provided her blood for a transfusion. It was too early to tell if it would help. They were grasping at straws. By all odds, Bill should be dead. There was nothing to do but wait. In the compound yard below, Everley Hayes and Jessie Green felt the same helplessness.

The crowd outside the clinic walls continued to grow and wait patiently. A few minutes before, Jessie had stepped to the gate to assure them Waa I Saang was still alive. All that could be done had been done. They could only pray and wait. William Newbern led his group in prayer on "the hill." The nuns and priests prayed at the convent outside Wuzhou. They counted Bill as a brother and an angel of mercy.

Everley Hayes suddenly realized she was extremely tired. The transfusion had weakened her. God grant that her blood would help! The hours since her arrival had passed very slowly. She sat down on a step, wearily. The Chinese knew how to wait. She would learn.

Late the next day, Sam Rankin had dozed off in a chair by Bill's bed. He awoke with a start. For a minute he watched Miss Lam, the surgical nurse. She masked her concern well, but he felt it.

Suddenly, she turned to him. "Is he not cooler?"

Quickly, Sam rose and felt Bill's forehead. Then he grasped his hand. "I believe he is!" His fingers felt Bill's pulse. "The fever has broken! He is going to make it!"

It is unbelievable how fast the news traveled.

Almost as soon as Sam's words of relief and victory were spoken, a glad cry arose from below.

Waa I Saang would live!

Sam watched the hills of Wuzhou recede as the Guangzhou ferry plowed through the waters of the West River. Bill Wallace was on the road to recovery. Now Sam, Everley Hayes, and Don Moore were returning to language school.

"I still don't see how he pulled through," Sam said. "There was no earthly reason for it."

Everley smiled, "No earthly reason, true, but maybe there was a divine reason."

In the fall of that year, 1948, Bill was back at work. He was still thin but fully recovered. He was no longer alone. The Rankins, the Galloways, and Everley Hayes had completed language training and moved to Wuzhou. Bill was never happier.

Chapter 34: Bill Makes Mission Trips

Bill and Sam enjoyed working together. They made an excellent team. Sam was impressed by Bill's surgical skills. He watched Bill carefully at every opportunity.

"Sam, come over here and meet my friend." Bill stood by a window with a filthy young boy. Sam recognized the boy as a beggar. Other boys often bullied him because he had a disability.

The Chinese boy's eyes darted fearfully from one doctor to the other. Life had not been kind to him. Because of his disability, he roamed the streets unwanted, teased, and unable to explain what he needed.

In the light from the window, Bill was looking at the boy's deformed mouth. His hand gently cupped the boy's chin.

"Let's fix him up, Sam. Let's give him a chance in life."

Sam moved in for a closer look, and Bill asked, "Have you ever done one of these?"

"No, I never have," answered the new missionary.

"You do this one," Bill said. "I'll assist you."

Under Bill's guidance, Sam did his first harelip and cleft palate surgery. The result was beautiful. The boy's eyes shone when he saw his new look in the mirror. When he could make himself understood for the first time, he cried with joy. Sam was elated, and Bill was excited to see Sam respond to the possibilities of a medical ministry in a place like Wuzhou.

When the boy was pronounced healed, he was discharged. Bill hired him as an orderly. He made a good one. He was especially good at reassuring fearful patients who faced surgery. Sam took note of Bill's interest and insight into the needs of the whole man.

Although Bill was only forty years old in 1948, he was a father to his staff. He was even asked more than once to stand up as father when one of them married. None of those present ever forgot a wedding that fall when an orphan girl, literally raised in the hospital and later trained as a nurse, was given in marriage.

Bill Wallace took the traditional role as if he indeed were her father. He worked out all the details a typical Chinese father would have managed. At the wedding feast, he was a typical father-of-the-bride and enjoyed himself immensely. New missionaries marveled at the acceptance he had among his adopted people.

With the enlarged staff to ease the hospital routine, Bill began to travel into nearby villages with missionaries who were

sharing the gospel. In October he took a
team to the little village of Hu Ching. They
moved through the streets of Wuzhou just
before dawn, carrying medical supplies, food,
clothing, Bibles, and gospel tracts. Bill owned
a new plywood boat and a powerful outboard
motor. He rigged up an awning and a towline
to carry the evangelistic team and supplies.
Twelve workers, medical and evangelistic,
volunteered for the trip.

It was barely dawn when they chugged
out on the glassy West River for a ten-mile ride
up the Fu River. The remainder of the trip had
to be made on foot.

When they reached the trail, Bill and the
team pulled the boats to the bank. Everyone
loaded equipment on his back. Then, they
climbed a towering green hill by a steep,
narrow path. On the other side of the hill they
gazed down into a peaceful valley. They spotted
the little village that was their destination.
As they started down the hill, children began
running from the village to meet them. Soon
they crowded about the missionaries shouting
greetings. Several who had come to know him
at the children's ward of the Stout Memorial
Hospital literally threw themselves at Bill.

Bill loved these mission trips. He liked
to walk into the village, greet the people and
ruffle the hair of the children. On these trips,
the Wuzhou workers distributed clothing,
New Testaments, and tracts. Members of
the evangelistic team went into the homes
and spoke to people they had met on other
trips. They also instructed new Christians

and worked with the local pastor. While they were doing this work, Bill and Everley Hayes conducted a clinic in another part of the village. Most of the patients were mothers and children. Bill and Everley gave them shots or cleaned and dressed their wounds. As Bill worked, children crowded around him and asked questions. When he looked up and responded in his Cantonese with its Tennessee drawl, they laughed and ran off. But they soon came back. They loved him and watched wide-eyed as he worked with patients.

Later, the missionary team gathered together for a service that began with the children singing Christian hymns in Cantonese. After a sermon and a closing prayer, the missionaries packed up to leave. The children escorted them to the edge of town singing, "God Will Take Care of You." Its melody was still ringing from the village when the missionaries topped the green hill.

Chapter 35: The Communists March

Christmas 1948 was a special time for the missionaries in Wuzhou and the staff of the Stout Memorial Hospital. For one thing, Bill and the nurses now had a family. Bill had "adopted" a child whose mother had died in the hospital. He named the boy, Paul. The nurses did most of the caring for him, but Bill felt very responsible for the little boy.

Bill liked to give some little gift to nearly everyone he worked with, and especially to the children in the hospital. Now, the Rankins, the Galloways and Everley Hayes were part of Bill's family. Christmas Eve was exciting. The missionary staff gathered together for dinner at the home of the Rankins. The night before, they had their Christmas program at the hospital. They exchanged gifts and had a service in the chapel to give thanks. Then, they had a party on the hospital terrace with choirs from the Baptist Bible school and the Alliance Bible school. The two groups sang Christmas songs with the student nurses' choir.

The next morning, shortly after finishing his rounds at six o'clock, Bill surprised Everley by suggesting they go over to "the hill" to wish the Alliance missionaries and his friend William Newbern a Merry Christmas.

"But they won't even be up yet!" she exclaimed.

"That's the whole idea," he replied with a mischievous grin.

After they finished checking the night reports, they walked down the empty Wuzhou streets and caught a small boat across the Fu River. They climbed the hill to the Alliance station. Only the dogs greeted them. Bill called a cheerful "Merry Christmas!" as loud as he could. Lights came on all over the compound. The Newberns loved Bill as if he were a part of their family. Bill felt the same way about the Newberns. Bill and Everley stayed for breakfast.

On January 17, the whole Baptist mission and the group from "the Hill" came to the Rankins' to celebrate Bill's forty-first birthday. He had been in China for fourteen years. Everley baked a birthday cake. The weather was gloomy and a very chilly 36 degrees. The missionaries enjoyed teasing Bill about being a bachelor at his age. They teased him because of something that happened just before Christmas.

One of Bill's close Chinese friends asked him for the umpteenth time why he did not marry. Bill replied jokingly, "Nobody will have me."

The Chinese friend was very concerned. "Would you like for me to get you a wife?"

Bill just grunted, hoping the question would go away. The sound he made meant "yes" to the Chinese. To Bill's horror, the Chinese friend appeared at the hospital the next day with a German-Chinese girl, a Eurasian, along with her mother, to arrange for her to marry Bill. Bill realized what was happening when the mother came in and gave him a hug. Then she began talking about a contract for the marriage.

Bill's face turned red. He said, "There must be some mistake."

She said, "Oh, no. I am sure there has been no mistake."

Suddenly, he remembered an emergency at the hospital and rushed away.

The mother returned often with her lovely daughter, but somehow she could never find Bill. He went for many long walks in the hills those days. It was only after a careful explanation by some of his friends, who tried hard not laugh, that the mother understood Bill was not going to marry her daughter!

The calm days at the mission after the Japanese War passed quickly. It seemed they were the calm before the storm. To the north, Communism was beginning to take shape and was on the move. The Communists were not strangers to Bill. They had been fighting Chiang Kai-shek and his Nationalists when Bill first came to China.

Communism had come from Russia to China in the 1920s. From 1921 to 1927 the

Communist Party, fed by Russia, grew from fifty thousand to two million trade union workers and nine million peasants. In the days of Sun Yat-sen, the first provisional president of the Republic of China, they gained a voice in government.

When Chiang Kai-shek took over China in 1925, however, he realized how dangerous the Communists were. He made a dramatic break with them. The Communists fought back, and Chiang Kai-shek began an all-out campaign to get rid of the Communist influence in China. By 1936 this effort was nearing success. Then the Communists kidnapped Chiang Kai-shek. This, together with the Japanese threat, allowed them to sign a treaty with the Chinese leader. Though the Japanese drive cut the Communists off from the rest of China, it gave them unlimited control of the north. There they strengthened their armies, trained many political workers, and began to infiltrate the rest of China under the cover of World War II.

Bill remembered how easily he dismissed Dr. Beddoe's predictions about the Russian threat. Russia had joined the Japanese War a few days before it ended. When the treaties were made, Russia turned over Manchuria to the Chinese Communists.

"We will live to regret this day," Dr. Beddoe said at the time.

When Nationalist troops were airlifted to the area, they found the Communists armed, fed, and waiting.

Early efforts by the United States

to stall the civil war in China only gave the Communists time to prepare. By late 1948 the issue was no longer in doubt. Chiang Kai-shek tried hard to fix corruption in his own party and deal with a poor economy. Still, Communism began a strong march to take over the Chinese government.

The missionaries gathered on the hospital porch to watch the Chinese New Year on January 28, 1949. Bill, Everley, and Miss Bradley were up until 2 a.m. delivering a baby. They went back out on the porch to watch the last part of the celebration. It continued into the wee hours of the morning.

The fogs were forming on the river when Bill said, "I am afraid things are going to change drastically before we see another of these celebrations."

In February, both the Nationalist capital at Nanjing and Chiang Kai-shek moved to Taiwan. Since the Chinese Communists demanded unconditional surrender, the last hopes for negotiations passed. It was a confused situation. The missionaries were uncertain about what might happen. They prayed and prepared themselves for whatever might come.

Chapter 36: Tough Decisions

It was spring 1949, and Guilin was threatened. Shanghai would soon fall. The Communist drive toward Guangzhou was making progress. The word from missionaries who were trying to stay on in Communist territory was not encouraging.

Ed Galloway and Bill decided to risk a trip to Hong Kong before the rainy season arrived. They needed to pick up an elevator a church in the U.S. had shipped to the hospital. It was a dangerous trip because advance Communist troops were now being seen along the West River. One week before, Ed had made the same trip. On his return voyage, Communists fired at his boat from the adjoining hills. Ed had looked up to find the man next to him dead, shot through the head.

As they approached the danger area on this trip, one of the ferry's crew members came up to Ed.

"Are you with him?" The man was

pointing at Bill, seated low against a railing, watching the foreboding banks.

Puzzled, Ed replied, "Yes, I am. Why do you ask?"

"The captain would like both of you to come to his cabin," the man said. "Please follow me."

Catching Bill's eye and motioning for him to come along, Ed followed. Inside the captain's spacious quarters, the crewman asked them to wait and excused himself. In a moment the captain entered. He addressed himself to Ed.

"Your traveling companion has saved my worthless life three times" the captain nodded toward Bill. "But he has refused to let me repay him. Now you are my guests, and I want you to share my meal with me. You will be safe here if the Communists fire on us again."

Smiling, the captain pointed to an armored dome over the cabin. "This way I shall repay the good doctor."

"Well, I'll declare!" exclaimed Ed, turning to look at Bill.

A bit embarrassed by the whole thing, Bill grinned. Then, he joked, "I was hoping to get credit for this one in heaven, but it looks as if we had better take it now."

They enjoyed the captain's hospitality. When a few random shots plowed into the boat a half hour later, they were grateful for the Chinese skipper's sense of honor.

When they returned to Wuzhou, Bill and Ed were met by a missionary couple from the hospital in Guilin. They were on their way to Hong Kong. They said the Communists were nearing Guilin. From all they could hear, prospects for continued missionary service under Communist rule were not good. The couple had decided to return to the United States.

The next few days were filled with rumors that the Nationalists had surrendered and that the Communists were within miles of the city. Bill and his fellow missionaries knew this was false. But they became concerned when the American consul in Guangzhou advised all Americans to leave South China as soon as possible. They realized it was time to take a hard look at the future.

Baker James Cauthen was now area secretary in the Orient for the Southern Baptist Foreign Mission Board. He was a former Guilin missionary. In May, Cauthen called a mission meeting in Guangzhou to study the situation. Bill and his fellow missionaries in Wuzhou selected Ed Galloway to go as their representative.

When Ed returned, they gathered in Sam Rankin's living room to hear his report. Dr. Cauthen's statement had been simple and to the point, Ed said. The area secretary shared decisions already made by missionaries in the north. He also talked some about what those who had decided to stay in Communist areas were experiencing. All were finding it difficult, but some felt it was worth trying.

Now they must decide to stay, to return home, or to transfer to another field. Cauthen pointed out that negotiations were under way to begin work in several new areas. Whatever they decided, the Board would back them completely. If they chose to stay, it must be because they definitely felt it was what God wanted them to do. There was to be no time limit on decisions, though with the Communist advance, they would need to decide soon.

When Ed concluded his report, the missionaries were silent for a moment. Then Bill spoke quietly, but firmly.

"This cannot be a station decision. It must be made individually. Each of us will have unique considerations, and each must decide now to respect the other's conclusion, no matter what it is."

It was the only approach to take. In the days that followed, they gradually made their choices. For some, the right choice seemed obvious. For others, it came only after much prayer and thinking about the consequences.

During this time, they listened carefully for word coming from other areas and the decisions others were making. In some places, the missionaries were asked by their Chinese friends to leave. There was the possibility that the presence of foreigners would might hurt what the Chinese Christians were trying to do. News from areas where Communists were already present seemed to support this action. If the Chinese Christians in Wuzhou felt this way, they did not share it with the Americans at this time. Had they done so, it might have made some decisions easier. Bill announced his decision first. He would stay. Too much was at stake to leave the hospital at this time. He was the logical person to stay with it.

Blanche Bradley was near retirement. Trained for Mandarin-speaking work and unable to speak the Cantonese dialect very well, she felt she would slow work down. She would go.

Ed and Betty Galloway decided to go. They had sn opportunity to begin work in Thailand among the Chinese people there. They felt they should take it. Their missionary career was just beginning, and they hoped for a more stable situation.

Jessie Green was due for time in the U.S., but she decided to postpone it and try to stay on. Her work was growing. She felt if she left at this time, she might not be able to get back in later.

Everley Hayes shared her decision with Bill after surgery one day. ''I'm going to stay on, Bill. The hospital needs a missionary nurse, and I'm just now getting to where I can handle the language pretty well.''

Bill smiled at the determined nurse. "I figured you would, Everley." Then, more seriously, he added, "You're sure this is what you really want to do? It may get pretty rough."

"I'm sure," she said. "I'm real sure."

Sam and Miriam Rankin finally made a difficult decision to go. Their youngest child needed a type of surgery done best in the States. They would go and hope another opportunity would open later.

That was it. Five would go. Three would stay. There was warm support for each decision.

Chapter 37: Missionaries Leave

The Galloways were the first to leave. The day they left on the ferry for Hong Kong, Bill and Ed walked up the hill back of the hospital.

"I know this is what we should do, Bill. The prospects at Bangkok sound good. The thing that bothers me is leaving you and Everley and Jessie. Now and then, I wonder if I'm running out on you."

Bill replied, "No. I definitely feel you are doing the right thing. You have a family, and you must take their well-being into consideration. If you stayed, you would be worried for them, and you would not be able to do the job you will be free to do in Thailand. With me, it's different. I'm the one to stay. I'm just one piece of man without other responsibilities."

"One piece of man" was an old Chinese saying used courteously to lessen one's value. It indicated a single, unencumbered, expendable person. By it, Bill meant his life was the only one at stake. He was the one prepared by God for this moment. He was the one to stay on in the face of the unknown. He would give the Stout Memorial Hospital and the Baptist witness every chance to continue once the Communists arrived.

"I'm just one piece of man … ," Ed Galloway repeated the conversation to his wife on the ferry to Hong Kong. "He really meant it. He has no concept of his own worth, and no worry for the future that I can see."

A few days later one of the Catholic missionaries dropped by the hospital for some medicine and stopped to visit with Bill.

"They tell me you are going to try to stay on, Bill."

"Why, yes, Father. Your team is staying, too. Aren't you?"

"True, but then we are expendable," the priest joked. "Well, somebody has to stay to look after you."

They laughed together, thankful for an opportunity to relax. There was nothing heroic in Bill's decision. He felt the same sense of duty he had felt when the Japanese were storming through South China five years before.

Soon it was time for the Rankins and Miss Bradley to leave. The women wept softly as the men shook hands quietly. They had enjoyed working together and wished the situation were different.

"Maybe someday, Bill."

"God willing, Sam. Take care of yourself and take care of my little girl for me." Bill was extremely fond of the Rankin's daughter who they were taking home for surgery.

Bill, Everley, and Jessie stood at the dock until they lost sight of the ferry around the bend. Then, silently, they walked back to the hospital.

Their sadness grew two weeks later when William Newbern walked over to the Baptist compound to tell Bill that the Orient secretary for the Missionary Alliance group had ordered them to go to Hong Kong. After the Newbern family left, Bill found it hard to look across the river without feeling sad.

But there was lots of work to do. The hospital had a lot of patients. They were short on staff because many nursing students had gone home. Bill began buying up vital supplies to store and use when they would not have access to outside markets. The Bamboo Curtain, the name of the Communist takeover, had already fallen in North China. South China could expect the same fate.

Then nature complicated matters. The West and Fu Rivers flooded in early July 1949. Soon the flood waters reached Wuzhou. Bill had to wade through water ankle-deep to get to church on the second Sunday in July. When the worshipers came out, the water had climbed to the top steps. Bill took a small boat back to the hospital.

By evening the water was at the doors of the clinic. Bill knew they were in for the worst flood in his sixteen years in China. The next morning, they stopped using the clinic and moved the equipment up to the hospital.

The muddy water stretched from the hospital grounds all the way to the far side of the valley. Much of Wuzhou was now underwater. Dr. Beddoe had always said it would never reach the hospital steps. Just as Bill decided Dr. Beddoe was going to be wrong for a change, the waters began to recede.

The retreating flood left a trail of destruction. Mud, slime, crumpled homes, and mangled trees were everywhere. The flood also brought disease. But the Chinese had crawled out of such disasters before to rebuild. This time was no exception. At the hospital, Bill faced the problem of no water. Their well had caved in. They also had no electricity and many flood victims seeking treatment. But the hard work was almost a blessing. It kept their minds off the Communist advance.

After the flood, the South China Mission decided to have its regular mission meeting in Guangzhou despite the small number of missionaries left. Fortunately, the unusual floods temporarily halted the Communists. Bill, Everley, and Jessie all decided to attend the meeting. It would be the last opportunity to visit with their fellow missionaries. The prospect made them happy. On the day they were to leave, however, Bill had to perform an emergency surgery. He sent the women on alone. He was very disappointed, but there was no question about where he belonged. He wrote a brief note for Everley to take to Gene and Louise Hill, who were staying in Guangzhou. It might be a long time before he got to see them again.

Bill worked steadily while his nurses were at the mission conference. On the afternoon they were to return, he decided to meet their plane. As he started to his bungalow for a shower and change of clothes, he saw the hospital business manager running up the path.

"Waa I Saang! Waa I Saang!"

"What's the problem, Chan?"

"Word has come that the Communists shot down the Guangzhou plane about a half hour ago! The pilot radioed they were being attacked. There has been no further communication."

Bill's heart pounded. "O God, please let them be all right," he prayed.

He was not sure he could take it if anything happened to Everley and Jessie. He started toward the gate on the run.

"Where are you going?" Mr. Chan called.

"Down to customs. They may know something," he shouted back.

At customs, they had confirmed that the plane had indeed been downed. First word from the scene said all on board were lost. They were trying to get a passenger list from Guangzhou now.

Bill sat down to wait, praying over and over again, "God, let them be safe."

Two hours later, customs still did not have the passenger list, but Bill was standing up with tears running down his cheeks. He was reading a telegram Chan had brought him.

```
Missed plane. Will come
by ferry on Monday.
EVERLEY and JESSIE.
```

They arrived safely on Monday.

Chapter 38: Waiting Anxiously

After the mission meeting, Baker James Cauthen decided to make one last visit to the South China stations that would soon be cut off by the Communists. Despite the danger, he and his secretary, Lucy Smith, booked passage on the seaplane to Wuzhou.

On the trip from Hong Kong to Wuzhou, Dr. Cauthen peered out at the familiar South China landscape. He wondered how long he and those whom he was going to visit would continue to serve there. For a second time in a decade, war threatened to engulf them. First, it was the Japanese. Now, it was the Communists. How much time was left? Three weeks? Three months? Dr. Cauthen knew the Communists would eventually win. Memories of the reports from North China concerned him. He did not know what would happen in the days ahead.

Dr. Cauthen was eager to see Bill Wallace. Cauthen admired Bill's determination not to be driven out by the Communists, "to stay as long as I can serve." But he found himself breathing a prayer for Bill's safety. Then the seat belt sign flashed on, and he realized they were approaching Wuzhou.

He stepped off the plane and was greeted by the three Wuzhou missionaries. Bill hollered in his brand of Cantonese, "Taxi, mister?"

Laughing, Cauthen threw his raincoat and briefcase into Bill's boat. Then he helped Lucy Smith as they tried to balance themselves. Bill, Everley, and Jessie asked about the Rankins, Miss Bradley, and the Galloways. They were grateful to hear that all had headed back to the U.S.

Bill said, "They did a good job here, but this is no place for a family."

Later that evening while waiting for the others, Dr. Cauthen stood alone on the porch of the old Beddoe house. He watched a red glow crown the hospital as the sun set on the hills beyond. The brown stones took on a ruddy softness.

The sound of footsteps turned his attention to the walk. Everley Hayes, in a crisp white uniform, was coming from her apartment. The reds and blues in the garden behind her formed a colorful background.

"Well," he said, "you don't look like you have been on duty all day."

She shook her head and said, "I have, and all night, too. A soldier came in yesterday with gangrene. He had walked over a hundred miles. We tried all night to save him, and I think we have succeeded."

"That's wonderful!" Cauthen replied. Then, turning to look at the hospital again, he said, "Don't they call it 'The Life of China' ?"

Just then, Bill loped around the corner. His stethoscope was flopping from his coat. Cauthen joked, "Dr. Wallace, I presume."

Everley laughed and quipped, "You ought to feel honored, Dr. Cauthen. When Bill shows up for any meal other than Sunday dinner, it must be an occasion."

Bill pretended to look hurt and then said, "It has been a long time since Sunday. Let's eat!"

After dinner, the missionaries, with Dr. Cauthen, sat on the porch and discussed some of the problems they soon would face.

"One of the most sobering aspects of staying on is that you will not have the protection of the American consul. Our Government will not recognize the Communist regime."

Dr. Cauthen made the statement slowly. He paused to let it sink in.

Bill asked, "Are the Communists confiscating American property yet?"

"They have not taken over any mission property as such, but they are making more and more demands in some areas," Cauthen answered. "In one place, local Communist authorities are asking to hold the title and let our missionaries 'use' the property free of charge."

"That sounds to me as if they intend to take it over," Jessie said.

"They may be planning to do just

that," Dr. Cauthen replied. "But, if we remain firm, they might hold off for a while to avoid unfavorable world opinion."

Bill was sitting on the concrete floor with his back resting against the cool wall. He looked at the hospital, then asked, "Would we fare better if we turned the property over to the Leung Kwang Baptist Convention? Perhaps the Communists would be less interested in taking it over then."

This action had long been Robert Beddoe's dream. Bill had often pondered its merits.

"In the long run, that might be the best action, but right now foreign property holders are faring better than the Chinese," Cauthen responded.

He did not have to spell this out. Already, stories were seeping out to a shocked world.

"Ultimately, it's the Lord's property," Cauthen continued. "We will have to trust that He will use it for his glory, come what may."

They nodded. Bill added, "And ultimately, we are his people. Even without the American consul, we always have the Lord."

The next day, Bill, Everley, Jessie, and many of the Chinese Baptist leaders saw Cauthen and Lucy Smith to their plane for their return to Hong Kong. As Dr. Cauthen shook Bill's hand firmly, he said, "Remember, Bill, there are going to be a lot of people praying for you in the coming months."

"We're counting on it." Bill smiled.

Now began the long wait.

Bill had the advantage of waiting out the advance of an enemy before. He tried to reassure Everley and Jessie, but he understood from experience their worry about the unknown.

In Wuzhou, Communist political workers were infiltrating every area of life. From their "underground" headquarters, they claimed they were ready to take control of the city. They used fear on one hand and assurances on the other to confuse the people. It was especially hard on the Christians. They knew that Communist beliefs were opposed to all they stood for. Many of the leaders were deciding whether or not to leave.

Bill and all the church leaders were dealt a severe blow when one of the hospital Bible women, long a faithful worker, was caught in a major sin. The Communists pounced on this to discredit the hospital and the Christians. But in the midst of the scandal, the Wuzhou Baptists experienced one of their most fruitful seasons. They baptized nineteen new believers a week after the scandal broke. It was as if God had chosen their weakest moment, humanly speaking, to display His power in their lives. Bill, Everley, and Jessie drew strength from the turn of events.

To try to relieve the increasing tension among the hospital staff, Bill suggested regular outings and recreation. Again and again, he hitched up an old raft to the back of his boat and hauled the student nurses and staff members upriver to Chicken Basket Island for a picnic and swim. He even rigged up a water sled to pull for the younger staff members. The doctor laughingly steered the boat trying to throw them from the sled.

But his efforts to keep their minds off the approaching Communists were only partly successful. Nearly every day more students pulled out to return home or flee the country with their families. There seemed to be no end to the gnawing fear.

The Communists were advancing up the West River. By the end of October, people in Wuzhou were in a panic. Shops that usually stayed open until nine o'clock at night started closing before sundown. People on the streets became fewer. Thieves became bolder. The town still housed a large group of Nationalist soldiers. Many were living in tents by the river. Others were living in old buildings in the hills. The local Communists worked overtime spreading rumors and distrust in preparation for the take-over.

Rumors floated everywhere. There were always people ready to believe them. One night, Bill heard the hospital was going to be robbed by a large band of thieves. He was urged to hide everything of value. He replied there was little use to do so. Things hidden could always be found, or people could be tortured to tell. Nevertheless, Bill spent that night in the hospital, a lonesome guard. Nothing happened, but the panic grew.

Refugees were coming in from Guangzhou and other cities that had fallen to the Communists. They, along with Nationalist troops in retreat, made a steady procession through the town to the West. Evacuation plans were passed out by the Nationalist officials, but the hospital staff notified the officials they would not evacuate. Knowing that Dr. Wallace was going to stay made some of the people feel better.

By the end of October, Bill and Everley had no choice but to dismiss the nursing classes. They had only two students left. The night they closed classes they heard on the radio that Guilin to the northwest had been lost. That loss meant that Wuzhou was the last Southern Baptist mission station in all China that was still unoccupied by the Communists.

It had been five and a half months since the Rankins, Galloways and Miss Bradley left Wuzhou. At that time, many thought it would be only a matter of weeks until the Communists took over. Now, at a meeting of the hospital staff, a doctor asked Bill how long it would be. Bill said they could count on one month. He was right, to the very day. The Communists were just hours from Wuzhou on Thanksgiving Day, 1949.

Everley and Jessie fixed a traditional meal, and then the three missionaries sat out on the porch to talk. Rumors said the Nationalist troops were to pull out that night. One said they planned to burn the city rather than turn it over to the Communists. The citizens feared fire and robbery more than anything else. For the missionaries, the big fear was the overall uncertainty of the next few hours and days.

Everley mused out loud. "It is a funny

feeling, this waiting. It is sort of a detached feeling, as though we are not really a part of it, but just onlookers."

"The thing that bothers me most," said Jessie, "is the fear in the faces of the people."

"I know," replied Bill. "Mr. Chan came by this morning and said he had finally decided he must take his family out. He was going to stay, but today he looked pale with fear."

Far below them a column of Nationalist troops filed through the streets. They could hear the iron shoes of the pack mules clanking on the cobblestones.

"Listen." Bill cupped a hand to his ear. They heard the unmistakable chatter of machine gun bursts. "I believe we had better wait this one out at the hospital. We can watch from the roof."

Closing the house, they ran to the old building and mounted the steps to the roof. There Bill pointed to the hill to their left.

"l don't see anything." Everley strained her eyes in the direction he pointed. Then tracer bullets arched into the town from a clump of bamboo. She saw running, crouching Communist soldiers moving into Wuzhou.

Two hours later, long columns of the green-uniformed soldiers were winding into the city. Their tennis shoes hardly disturbed the silence or scuffed the dust. From the front of their soft caps, with earflaps tied over the top, gleamed a red star.

Wuzhou, the Stout Memorial Hospital, and the three remaining Southern Baptist missionaries were behind the Bamboo Curtain.

Chapter 39: Behind the Bamboo Curtain

Life under the Communists was relatively uncomplicated in the beginning. True to their pattern, they first tried to gain the people's confidence. The People's Party began organizing immediately, but most people, including the missionaries, were lulled into a false sense of security.

A real scare came to the hospital staff, however, the day after the Communist take-over. Bill was called out of surgery when a large group of soldiers started up the road toward the hospital. He met them at the clinic and learned they were demanding to be housed in the hospital. He politely pointed out that patients were housed in the hospital. Staff were not authorized to run a boarding house. The officer in charge made a few thinly veiled threats, so Bill agreed to furnish them temporary space on the first floor.

The nurses, especially those sleeping in the single nurses' quarters, were scared.

Everley moved in with them from her house in the compound. She was not sure what protection she would be, but it seemed to give them confidence. Bill moved a cot to the top of the steps between the first and second floors. Any of his "boarders" would have to step over him to get to the second floor.

Resolved, but not disrespectful, Bill's manner spoke courage. The soldiers respected him. They were also under orders to be on their best behavior. The Communists used courtesy to their advantage during the early days. The soldiers stayed at the hospital only one night and then moved on.

"It's impossible." Everley Hayes said to the Communist official. As Bill came up to the nurse's desk, he noticed Everley with her hands on her hips.

"What's the matter, Everley?"

"This man wants me to send ten nurses in full uniform to a parade in one hour. I can't do it. I'm shorthanded as it is. We're a hospital, not a marching unit."

The official smiled, but his smile was forced and icy. "This hospital must cooperate with the People's Party if it expects the Party to sanction it and protect it. Your cooperation will prove your goodwill."

Everley started to reply, but Bill restrained her. Then he said, "Our hospital will be represented in the parade."

The official bowed and departed. As he left, Everley turned to the doctor, obviously puzzled. "Where in the world ... ?" She did not finish.

He grinned and said, "Send four nurses. We can cover for them for a few hours, and we do want to show our goodwill."

"He said ten!" she protested.

"But I only said we would be represented ... "

"Shhh!" Everley stopped the doctor. She waited for an orderly to move by. He had been furiously dusting only a few feet away.

"I don't trust that new orderly. He always listens in on everything. He is giving the nurses the creeps. Do you think he could be here as an informer?" Everley asked the question cautiously, a bit fearfully.

Bill rubbed his chin thoughtfully. "Maybe, Everley. They seem to have infiltrated everything and every place. Chan says the walls now have ears. Let's make it a point to be sure we're alone when we are referring to anything political."

The next day they read in the paper of a "spontaneous parade" held in Wuzhou as proof of the new government's popularity. Mass meetings were interspersed with the "spontaneous" demonstrations. The Baptist church was commandeered for such a gathering one Wednesday afternoon shortly before its members were to meet for prayer. The distraught pastor came to Bill and asked him to come to the church. Bill explained to an official that a regular meeting was scheduled there. The official assured him it would be available at the time for their meeting.

The noisy meeting adjourned as promised at the time for prayer. The waiting worshipers entered and began their meeting. But they met in the midst of posters left intentionally from the Communist rally. They read, "China for the Chinese." "Foreigners Have Ruined China." "Chiang Kai-shek, the Butcher, Is a Foreign Dupe."

As the members bowed for prayer, no one mentioned the signs.

Life had changed for Bill and the other two missionaries, but more in atmosphere than routine. Their routine was the same. They healed and served in the name of their Lord. The people who needed their help did not stop coming.

Christmas 1949 was subdued. Jessie, Everley, and Bill gathered in the girls' quarters for a private Christmas dinner. It was a great contrast to the previous Christmas, when they had all been so happy. They had less to eat this time, but they still managed roast chicken, potatoes, and ice cream. There was no real shortage of food during those weeks, but they did not feel free to go out and do much purchasing. During dinner, Bill was extremely talkative. He tried to cheer up Jessie and Everley and create a festive atmosphere. Afterward, they knelt together in prayer.

The New Year brought more Communist festivities. Everyone was expected to participate. Despite Everley's protests, her nursing staff was taken again and again for demonstrations. Her students were also commandeered for Communist courses. Some of the nurses left the hospital to join the youth corps organized by the Communists. Others began to believe the Communist teaching. This strained things among those who were loyal to their Christian faith and did not feel they could reject God to accept the Party line.

Now the public trials began. First, only the most obvious tyrants were brought to trial. But the people were being schooled in a new type of trial, a trial by mob. They were commanded to appear before large open-air courts. Led by people planted in the crowd, the people learned to respond with cries and yells on signal.

The first trials in South China were for those guilty of the crime of being a landlord. Crowds were convened for the trials early in the morning. The leaders whipped them into a frenzy by singing Communist songs and chanting slogans.

When the landlords were brought up from jail, they were greeted by crowds with drums and cymbals. They marched the landlords along like animals in a circus parade. Their hands were tied behind their backs to make them look more like criminals. The Communists placed cone-shaped dunce caps on the landlords' heads.

Trials began with long speeches on democracy, the will of the people, and the judgment of the people. Then the accusers came. Often they were women who screamed and yelled the crimes of the landlords.

The leader asked the mob after each accusation, "Is that just?"

The mob yelled "NO!"

The leader then shouted, "Should he be

punished?"

The crowd screamed, "YES!"

In the midst of this madness, the gospel of Christ was preached at Stout Memorial Hospital. Bill and his staff dedicated themselves to mercy rather than to murder and to peace rather than to rioting. It was a marked contrast to Communist rule.

But the conditions under which they worked grew more and more difficult. Bill tried to keep busy in the clinic with medical experiments and surgery. He had an unusual number of stomach ulcer cases. Tension was mounting. Fear was taking its toll. Word came of more missionaries leaving. Eugene Hill became seriously ill with a hemorrhaging ulcer and was ordered out of China. After weeks of waiting for an exit permit, he and his wife and small son made their way to Hong Kong and back to the States. Bill breathed a prayer of gratitude when he heard they were safely out.

Then the Wuzhou Christians suggested Jessie should leave. While Everley and Bill were involved primarily in medicine, Jessie was involved strictly in sharing the gospel. It was becoming so difficult to hold Christian meetings they advised Jessie to leave for her own good as well as for theirs. She reluctantly applied for her permit to leave. It was granted several weeks later, and she made her way out. This left only Bill and Everley.

It was a trying time for the doctor and his nurse. They needed each other's company more than ever before, but they had less opportunity to be together. They were able to be together only in social functions with others present. The Communists were quick to accuse foreigners of sin at the slightest opportunity. As a result, Bill and Everley "avoided all appearance of evil." Except for dinners with the staff, they took their meals separately and met only in terms of the routine of the hospital. They understood the necessity, and they were willing to pay the price to keep from hurting their witness among the people.

But one day Bill walked out of intricate surgery, peeled off his rubber gloves, laid aside his operating gown, and asked Everley to go for a walk along the river. She knew why he had chosen that particular time. It was still before three o'clock in the afternoon. For about three hours, there would be a lot of activity along the streets and the riverbanks and the roads. There would be no opportunity for them to be out of anybody's sight and give anyone reason to talk.

Smiling, she said, "Let's go."

At first they just walked quietly. Everley noticed Bill was beginning to show his forty years for the first time. His hair had thinned, and since his brush with death three years previously, he had kept it clipped short. Now there was a hint of gray in it. Lines creased his forehead. The corners of his eyes, which had so often been creased by grinning, even now held the hint of a grin. Things were more subdued, but daily activities in the streets of Wuzhou had not really changed.

Lean, brown boys pushed crude-wheeled carts piled high with sacks of grain or charcoal down the streets. Red paper lanterns scrawled with advertising still hung in store fronts to welcome customers. The smell of dried fish filled the air, and, since it was summertime, the smell was strong. The Chinese wore their black summer suits of silk lacquered on the outside. They contrasted sharply with the white uniforms of the two missionaries who walked among them.

The missionaries walked by the Baptist True Light Book Store, now closed by the Communists. They saw an emblazoned Communist banner across the front of the church. It was going to be used for a Communist rally denouncing something or someone. Dusty-legged old men with white beards and pale eyes crouched behind baskets of dried persimmons, eating with chopsticks and glancing disinterestedly at the Americans.

At the edge of town, the missionaries walked along the riverbank, every now and then coming under towering bamboo or great banyan trees. Boatloads of wood floated along the river. Smaller boats closer to shore moved in aimless patterns. Bill and Everley noticed that people did not talk to them as readily as they once had. Yet, some whom Bill had treated at the hospital waved briefly.

The two kept walking. Farther up the river, they passed a little group of shacks with children playing in the front. Bill grinned at the children, and they returned his smiles. Then an older one spoke loudly from behind a fence made of crates, "Look out for the foreign devils!" The children scattered.

All this time they had been quiet. Now

Bill began to talk. He talked as if he knew things were drawing to a close.

"You know, Everley, someday we will have done all we can do here. We may have to look for another place to work."

She nodded and pulled at a young bamboo stalk beside the walk.

"I have been doing a lot of thinking about it lately. It seems to me there are some places where medical missionaries could be the key to some otherwise locked doors," Bill continued.

Reaching down, he picked up a rock and flicked it out into the river. He laughed at himself as he remembered doing that before. It seemed a long time ago and a long way off.

"I have been thinking about the South Sea Islands. Java, Sumatra, and Borneo are all places where a medical mission program might be used to begin Baptist work. I think a hospital can get us into areas we cannot enter otherwise. I've heard that Peter Parker opened China at the point of his lancet. Southern Baptists are going to go into those other areas someday. They are going to have to have someplace to put all the China missionaries. And, I'm not quite ready to retire yet."

Everley grinned at him. He still looked young, despite the signs of age that had appeared recently. She could not think of him as at the end of his ministry, by retirement or anything else.

"Yes, I think we could begin a good work in that area," she said. "Maybe we could get Sam and Miriam Rankin and Betty and Ed

Galloway to help us out there."

At the thought of their departed colleagues, they fell silent. The conversation lagged. When she spoke again, Everley turned to their immediate plans. The staff needed some diversion. With tension building up all around them and yet so much being required of them, Bill admitted it would be good to get away. They decided on another boat trip. Bill would take his boat and pull a good-sized barge that would carry all the staff that could be spared. They would take along the surfboard and a lot of fried chicken and find a good swimming place. With that resolved, they returned to the compound, their separate residences, and their work.

The outing went well. Everyone was looking for something to take their minds off their circumstances. Many of the nurses were finding themselves torn between Communist propaganda and the Christian doctrines of the hospital and the missionaries that meant so much to them.

Bill enjoyed himself. He operated the boat when the others were surfboarding. When they were swimming, he lay on the bank lazily scratching the back of his dog's neck. His thoughts were far away.

Chapter 40: To Live is Christ

The crisis that came in July 1950 seemed to be related directly to the Korean conflict. When the North Korean invasion of South Korea began, Communist propaganda called "American Imperialists" the real villains. Despite the fact the North Koreans started the attack, the South Koreans and their American allies were pictured as aggressors. This propaganda affected Bill and Everley and all who were associated with them.

When the United Nations entered the conflict in late July, the situation became even more difficult. New sets of regulations were published by the Communists. Tolerance and restraint began to disappear. They had served their purpose. Now the real face of Communism surfaced. The new look started wholesale arrests. Guilty or suspect, masses of people were thrown into jail.

Bill received a group of Chinese Communist officials at the hospital. They

notified him of an expensive tax that would
be imposed on the hospital. Bill decided that
agreeing to the tax, even if the hospital could
afford to pay, would be playing into Communist
hands. So, he steadfastly refused. He said he
would appeal it to their supervisors and that
it was illegal. He said he did not believe the
People's Government would hurt an institution
that provided good to the people. He knew
better, but his insistence threw them off guard.

The people were afraid they would
lose Waa I Saang if something were not
done. Local citizens gathered a petition from
leading people of Wuzhou. They took it to
the People's Government headquarters at
Guangzhou. The Communists there evidently
felt the time was not yet ripe for a showdown.
They granted an exemption from the tax. But
the local Communists and their superiors in
Guangzhou now knew how much influence Bill,
an American, had in Wuzhou. The Communists
were planning to invade Korea in support
of the North Koreans and to oppose the
Americans and the United Nations. In early fall
a hate-America campaign reached a frenzy in
Wuzhou.

At rallies, Communist leaders began to
denounce America and American "exploiters."
They called them Yankee dogs, imperialist
wolves, and capitalistic dogs. The problem
with this strategy in Wuzhou was that the
only American most of these Chinese knew
was Bill Wallace. His life and the impact of his
ministry made the charges against America
and Americans seem incredible to them.

Stout Memorial was an American hospital that had treated the illnesses of many people in Wuzhou. The Americans there, in spite of the risk and danger to themselves, identified themselves with the Chinese, rich or poor. Bill was an American. He was the finest surgeon in all China. He was a hero of the Japanese War. He loved their children, and he had lived a good life among them for fifteen years.

Because Bill was so highly thought of, the Communist leaders began to look for ways to undermine his influence. His life and testimony threatened their agenda. Finally, it was decided that the only way to discredit the hospital and the American Christians it represented was to discredit Bill. They put their plans into action against him in early December when China joined the Korean War. The Communist party began purging China of American interests and influential Americans across the nation. What happened to Bill was not isolated.

Chapter 41: Bill is Arrested

The evening of December 18, Bill completed his rounds at the hospital as usual. A young Communist soldier with a ruptured appendix seemed to be recovering well, but Bill checked anyway. An elderly woman who had surgery to remove a gallstone two days before was holding her own. The doctor stopped by the night nurses' desk and jotted down some instructions for special care. No matter how full the hospital, he assumed primary responsibility for every patient's welfare.

Stretching his long frame, he yawned, rubbed his eyes, excused himself, and walked into the chill night air. At the gate of the clinic, he stopped and looked out over the blinking lights of Wuzhou. It had rained off and on most of the day. A misty fog gave an eerie feel to the scene. Bill could not quite shake off the sense of impending disaster.

Though the hospital had secured registration, he was not sure how much that would mean. The Communists continued to claim foreign property and institutions of all kinds. Now that the Chinese were at war with the United Nations and America, how long could the mission hospital be allowed to serve? Perhaps it was time to leave China. He turned and looked back to the lights of the hospital that gleamed over the city as lights of hope. Still he had opportunity to heal and alleviate suffering. Could he run out on that?

He started over to see Everley and the senior nurse, Miss Luk, but suddenly realized how exhausted he was. Instead, he returned to his bungalow. He expected to be called during the night for a troublesome case. He decided to sleep while he could.

The doctor's housekeeper saw Bill approaching. The housekeeper noticed how tired Bill looked. His hair was gray, and the lines of his face were deeper. The houseboy worried about the doctor who so seldom thought of himself.

"Hello, Rastus. It's a good day for ducks," Bill said. He had nicknamed the houseboy, Rastus.

It occurred to Bill that Rastus probably wouldn't understand that, but then he was too tired to care.

"Greetings, Waa I Saang. I will have you some milk and bread very shortly."

"Just bring it into my room, Rastus. I am very tired," Bill said.

"Ah, you have had a hard day. You must sleep through the night for a change."

Bill looked at him kindly and said,

"Rastus, when you say your prayers tonight, you might mention that to the good Lord. I think it would be fine to sleep all night for a change."

After a big glass of milk and a half-dozen slices of bread with a little butter, Bill stretched out on his small bunk. As he lay there with his head pillowed on his arm, he tried to understand what was bothering him. He was not exactly afraid. Goodness knows, he had a lot more to be afraid of many times before, but something made him uneasy.

About three o'clock the next morning, Chinese Communist soldiers brought a dozen young teachers to a small meeting room near the center of Wuzhou. There a local People's Republic official briefed them on their responsibility. They were going to search the headquarters and arrest Dr. William Wallace, who was, they claimed, "President Truman's chief spy in Wuzhou."

"Ai," murmured the teachers. They knew Dr. Wallace. Who would have thought he was a spy? But if the Government said so, it must be true.

Following the explanation, the teachers left with a group of thirty or more Communist soldiers. Silently, they moved through the streets of Wuzhou to the gates of the clinic of the Stout Memorial Hospital. As the rest of them melted into the shadows along the wall, one rapped on the door and said, "Let us in."

They could hear some fumbling inside and then a servant answered, "Who is there?"

The leader grinned at his hiding fellows

and answered, "We have a sick man here. Open up."

When the gates swung open, the soldiers quickly pushed aside the frightened servant. They went throughout the compound according to their assignments. Several soldiers surrounded the hospital. Others moved to each of the nearby bungalows. They woke up the people living there. Still others went to each of the hospital's floors and rounded up the staff.

In the bungalow where Bill was sleeping, Rastus woke up when he heard the noise. He ran to the door. As soon as he opened it, three soldiers burst inside. They rudely pushed him against the wall. They marched into Bill's room and ordered him from his bed. The soldiers then searched Bill's room. In a moment, they seemed satisfied. They ordered Bill and Rastus to the hospital. As they left, Rastus turned to lock the door. The official in charge would not allow him to do so.

When Bill stepped into the light of the fifth-floor room where the staff had been gathered, cries of concern and fear greeted him. They looked to him as children to a father. He quieted them with a word of assurance. Then walking to the front, he turned to face his accusers.

The officer in charge of the group was a young man. He said, "We know this is a den of spies. The People's Republic is aware that some of you are counterrevolutionaries. This will not be tolerated. Dr. Wallace, we know that you are President Truman's chief spy here in South China. You have been found out. You will no longer be able to carry on your clandestine activities."

A gasp of protest arose from the staff. "It is not true. Not Waa I Saang. No, you are wrong."

"Enough!" The harsh command from the unsmiling leader brought immediate silence. "We shall prove it to you. Either he has deceived you, too, or else," and he narrowed his eyes, "you are a part of his treasonous activities."

"We are what we seem to be." They all turned as Bill spoke in measured tones. "We are doctors and nurses and hospital staff engaged in healing the suffering and sick in the name of Jesus Christ. We are here for no other reason."

"Aha! You speak smoothly, but we expected as much. No matter. We shall see for ourselves the proof."

Looking around the room, he pointed out the hospital evangelist and the business manager. He told them they should witness the search. Then taking Bill and Rastus with them, the soldiers went downstairs and across to Bill's bungalow.

When they arrived, the soldiers began a search. They went directly to Bill's room. With mock surprise, they discovered a package under the doctor's bamboo bed mat. Hastily unwrapping the brown paper, the leader cried out, "Here is proof!" He held a small pistol.

Rastus, crying out in protest, said, "That was not here before."

The leader pushed Rastus roughly

against the wall, nearly throttling him with his forearm. He threatened him with the butt end of the pistol.

Bill spoke up and said, "That is not my gun. I do not own a gun. I do not know where that one came from."

The leader grinned at Bill. Then he barked orders for the house to be bolted and secured. He ordered that Bill be taken back to the hospital office. At the office, they informed Bill he was under arrest for suspicion of espionage. They said they were taking him to their headquarters for further questioning. The leader said he knew there was also wireless equipment around the hospital. They would search until they found it.

Meanwhile, Everley had been placed under house arrest. She was not allowed to talk to Bill. From her window, she saw the soldiers march Bill off between them for questioning. As they disappeared into the streets of Wuzhou, she had the strange feeling she would never see him again.

Chapter 42: To Die is Gain

Faced with wild charges of espionage and hints of other charges to come, the Communists put Bill in a cell. They left him alone for some time. He received meals from the hospital, and he told his jailer about Jesus Christ. He also preached from a cell window to two or three peasants who gathered to hear him. When the hospital staff heard this, they celebrated. Everley and the hospital administrator made formal requests for the release of the doctor. It was impossible for them to inform either the American consul or the Foreign Mission Board. They could only pray, and that they did.

A week after Bill's arrest, the Communists turned away Rastus when he brought Bill's food one morning. They said he would no longer be able to receive it. That night a called meeting was held at one of the big town halls in Wuzhou. All citizens of any importance were commanded to attend. There the man

who had arrested the doctor rose to inform the
crowd that Dr. William Wallace of the Stout
Memorial Hospital had confessed to being a
spy under the command of President Truman.

They talked about the gun and hinted
at dark deeds the doctor had done. They asked
for those who had any accusation against Dr.
Wallace to come forward with their charges.
None came. When the planted Communist
denouncers began to yell vindictive statements
against the doctor, they were surprised that the
crowd, despite their training, did not join them.
No one was deceived. The doctor was being
railroaded. Everyone knew it.

Bill's "confession" was a statement with
his name, age, length of service in China, and
other factual matters. Reading it and realizing
it was all true, he signed it. The Communists
then typed into a blank part of the paper the
statement that he had been sent to China
as a secret service man by the United States
Government. This was the confession.

The next day, the guards woke Bill up
early. They shoved him out into a courtyard.
He realized for the first time he was not the
only missionary being held. He recognized a
Catholic sister and a bishop. Grinning despite
the circumstances, he spoke to them. They
greeted each other warmly before the guards
rudely separated them.

The Communists took another step to
discredit the well-liked doctor. They placed a
sign with obscene accusations and charges over
his head. They tied his hands behind his back.
With others, they marched him through the

streets to the Fu River and across to the main
prison halfway up the hill. It was the same hill
he had visited many times before when the
Christian Missionary Alliance and his friend,
William Newbern, were there. On the way over,
he was shoved by a guard. He fell and badly
hurt a hand that he threw out to break his fall.
He received no care.

Daily, sometimes hourly, and often
through the night at the prison, guards would
wake him and bring him to an interrogator's
room. The world did not yet know about
brainwashing. The practice would be more fully
publicized after the Korean War. Bill Wallace
began to experience it the second week of his
imprisonment. The single-minded, sensitive
young doctor found that the Communists had
made up a long list of charges against him.

Their accusations upset Bill. They
shouted them over and over again, growing
louder and louder. They did not allow Bill to
defend himself. No excuses or answers were
permitted.

It overwhelmed him to hear accusations
of incompetence in surgery, of murdering and
maiming Chinese patients, of performing illegal
and obscene operations. His interrogators
hinted that doctors from all over China had
gathered evidence on him. They said these
doctors demanded his punishment. Eventually
they returned him to his cell. He was
exhausted. His cell was a bare room with a thin
pallet for protection from the damp and cold
and filth of the floor.

On another day, the guards gathered all

the foreign prisoners into an open courtyard.
One by one they forced the prisoners to stand
by a table piled high with guns, bullets, opium,
radios, and other items. The Communists
claimed they had confiscated them in the raids.
Then the guards photographed each prisoner
behind the table. When it came Bill's turn to
step up to the table, the guard behind him
almost pushed him into it. Rudely, they posed
him with the antennae of a radio to prove the
spying charges.

The Catholic missionaries who were in
prison with Bill, and who were later released,
knew Bill was shaken by the interrogations.
The rest of that day, the Communists gathered
the prisoners in front of a large crowd of
Communist soldiers. The soldiers mocked
and beat the missionaries. Toward the end
of the day, one of the missionaries found an
opportunity ask Bill how he was holding up.

Managing a weak grin, he replied, "All
right. Trusting in the Lord."

Bill Wallace was fighting the battle of his
life. The battle was not whether he could out
argue his accusers. He was not even equipped
to begin. It was not a battle of physical
endurance, though that would come soon. It
was a battle for sanity.

From his cell in the night, Bill
sometimes cried out in agony after the battle
was over. With pieces of paper and a smuggled
pencil, he wrote short affirmations to try to
keep his mind centered. Some were Scripture
passages. Others were simple denials of guilt.
He stuck these on the walls of his barren room

and repeated them to himself in an effort to prepare for the next interrogation.

But each one came like a high wave. At times, he was all but overwhelmed by the interrogation. Delirium, crying, and blank periods came, but he fought on, clinging to his faith. His fellow victims, not yet subjected to the intensive brainwashing, helplessly watched this inhuman assault on one of the greatest men they had ever known. Frantically, they tried to reach him from time to time by calling through their cells. But it was a lonely battle. Only Bill and the Lord who loved him could fight it.

Then something went wrong. The Communists plainly intended to brainwash Bill into an open confession. They wanted him to deny publicly everything he stood for. They thought they were close, but Bill's tough spirit would not give up easily. His protests rang through the night.

The guards, driven by fear or maybe guilt, came to his cell in the night with long poles. They cruelly thrust them between the cell bars to jab the doctor into unconsciousness. Somebody figured wrong. Though no one heard Bill Wallace cry, "It is finished," Bill's life on earth had come to an end. Quietly, his soul slipped from his torn body and his exhausted mind. He was with Jesus, the One He had so faithfully served. Bill Wallace was dead to the world, but he was alive forever with God. It was February 10, 1951.

The next morning the guards ran down the cellblock. They shouted that the doctor had hanged himself. They asked the two Catholic priests imprisoned there to come with them. They went into the cell where Bill's body was hanging from a beam by a rope of braided quilt. The guards tried to get the fathers to sign a statement that he had committed suicide. They would not do so. They finally signed a statement saying how they had found him. But they suspected that the Communists were trying to make a murder look like a suicide.

Back at the hospital, the staff had waited prayerfully through all the weeks of Bill's imprisonment. They received word to get the body of Dr. Wallace. Everley went with her housekeeper and another nurse. They would not let Everley go into the cell, but they let the housekeeper in. Everley instructed him quietly to be sure to note how the body looked. Bill's upper body was bruised, but he was missing the signs of hanging. The Communists had tried to cover up one botch with another, but they did not want Everley to see this.

The Communists provided a cheap wooden coffin. As soon as the body was ready, Communists soldiers put it in the coffin and nailed the coffin shut. The small group of hospital staff and the Communist soldiers set out for Wuzhou.

In a small leaking boat, they paddled downriver under bleak February skies. They came to the bamboo-shaded cemetery overlooking the river. A grave was dug, but no service was allowed. The Communist soldiers stayed until the last spade of dirt had been put in. Afterward, they drove everyone away. All that remained was the grave that marked the resting place of one of China's great Christian saints.

As the boats pulled away from the bank, Everley looked back at the scene. She was overwhelmed by the loneliness of Bill's final resting place.

It did not remain an unmarked grave for long. Bill's Chinese friends were shocked by the loss of the doctor who had lived only to serve them. No amount of Communist propaganda could make them believe he was anything other than what they had known him to be. Despite the danger involved, they collected a fund for a marker. They lovingly built a monument over the lonely grave.

They laid a cement terrace on the grave and another on the level below it. Concrete steps led from the lower terrace to the grave. Over it, they erected a single shaft reaching heavenward. On the shaft they inscribed in simple Scripture their estimate of the life of Dr. William L. Wallace: "For to Me to Live Is Christ."

Chapter 43: Sharing Bill's Story

Everley unfastened her seat belt and reached for her purse. She checked again to see if the little box was in the purse and then looked out the window at the approaching terminal building. Knoxville, Tennessee, was a new town to her, but she felt like she had been there before. It seemed strange that this was where Bill Wallace's life began. It seemed even stranger that it had ended in a small city in China.

As the plane taxied toward the gate, she rested her head back against the seat and tried to remember. Like still photos in a slideshow, she recalled the scenes the Stegalls would want to hear about: the hospital, the staff, Newbern, Rastus, Bill. She wanted to remember him laughing, making rounds, at the helm of his boat, roughing his beloved German shepherd, Duchess. For a while, especially during the six long months she was interned in Wuzhou, all she had remembered was his lean figure being led away into the darkness the night the Communists came and the cell where they claimed his body. Now she could remember the happier moments. Now she could visit the Stegalls.

Sydney and Ruth Lynn Stegall and their son embraced Everley as if she were a member of the family. During the long months since Bill's death, they had prayed for Everley's release and her safe return to the States. Somehow they could not lay their feelings to rest until they talked to her. There were too many things they had to know.

As Everley walked about the restful, tree-shaded Stegall yard, she remembered the time Bill told her of the place he called his permanent address. She and Bill had walked to the old Christian cemetery after a long surgical stint. They walked up the green hill and then down a winding green path where so many missionaries or their children were buried.

As they took the river path back, Bill talked about home. The brick patio, the barbecue pit, the dogwoods and maples, all were as he had described them. His vivid descriptions had given her the feeling she had actually been here.

Sydney Stegall interrupted her thoughts.

"William always slept on that breezeway when he was home on furloughs. He said it was more like home, though he missed his log pillow. One night for a joke I put some bricks under his pillow. The next morning Bill told me that he had the best night's sleep he'd had in weeks."

Everley laughed, "That sounds like him. He needed less to be comfortable than anyone I ever knew."

It was the first time they had mentioned Bill, and they all realized it. Ruth Lynn Stegall said, "There is so much we want to know, Everley. So very much."

Everley's eyes were full. "And there's a lot to tell."

After dinner, they settled back to talk. The Stegalls wanted to hear about her release from China first. Everley confessed that the six months between Bill's death and her release were terribly hard.

"I was actually afraid of losing my mind. The Communists would not let me leave my house and yard nor talk to any of the staff. From my window, I could see them passing to and from the hospital. Every now and then, they would cast fearful glances in my direction. Sometimes I waved, but they seldom responded. You never knew who might be a spy during those last months. This was one of the most nerve-racking things of the time under the Communists. Bill could deal with it when he was alive, but it bothered me.

"I played my piano and read and re-read a psychiatric textbook I had. I had to keep my attention on anything but Bill's death and my uncertain future. I prayed and read my Bible and asked God more than once, 'Why?'"

Sydney nodded. "We've asked that one ourselves."

Everley continued, "I applied at least once a week for permission to leave. All I got was the run-around. Then one day, they told me I had permission, but that I would have to leave within twenty-four hours. Also, I was to take out with me only the bare necessities."

She looked at them apologetically, "I really wanted to bring some of Bill's things, but they confiscated most of them. I was not allowed to go after the rest."

Ruth Lynn said, "Of course, we understand. We are just glad that you are here."

"I did manage to sneak this out, though." Everley dug the little box from her purse and opened it with care. From it, she extracted a small gold ring and handed it to Ruth Lynn.

"This was Bill's chop ring. We took it from his hand. I guess they overlooked it."

"Chop ring?" Ruth Lynn was puzzled by the term.

"It is a Chinese custom. A kind of signature ring. See, these characters stand for his name. In the old days, it was used to press into the wax that was sealing a letter."

"Why is the piece missing?" Sydney fingered the treasure. "Did you have to cut it off?"

"No." Everley smiled. "Bill said he used a piece of it to fill his tooth during the year he was refugeeing in western China."

They were silent for a moment.

"Everley, we believe that somehow God used Bill's death for His glory even as he used his life." Ruth Lynn spoke firmly. "We've heard from so many who have been inspired and encouraged by Bill's dedication that I have come to believe it was a part of God's plan for his life."

Sydney got up and went to a desk. "You ought to read some of the things people have said." Taking a stack of letters and clippings, he walked to Everley's side. "For instance, listen to this letter from Mr. Newbern."

They were quiet as he read.

> Bill's death was more
> than a shock to us. It
> left us with a deep sense
> of loss. … We cannot
> escape the impression
> that Bill felt he would
> be called to walk through
> 'the valley of the shadow
> of death.' He thought it
> was God's will. There
> have been and there will
> be many martyrs, but few
> can so glorify Him in
> death as Bill did.

Sydney continued, "Listen to this letter from a Swedish missionary who is serving in Indonesia now."

> He loved the Chinese
> enough to give his life
> for them, and they loved
> him enough to entrust
> their lives into his
> hands. His life has been
> a challenge to our lives.

Ruth Lynn said, "Read her the one from Dr. Rankin."

Sydney shuffled through the letters and then began reading again.

When God chooses someone
to make a superlative
witness of his love, he
chooses a superlative
child of his. He chose
his own Son, Jesus, to
make the witness on the
Cross. And now it seems
that he chose Bill to
make this witness. To
give his life in love and
service for the people
whom he served fits in
naturally with Bill's
life. The two things go
together because he was
that kind of man. His
life's service among men
bears out the testimony
of his death. Bill's
death was not the result
of his being caught by
a situation from which
he could not escape. He
deliberately chose his
course with a commitment
that made him ready to
take any consequences
that might come. He
followed the same course

when the Japanese armies
approached Wuzhou, and
he has followed it
throughout his missionary
service.

"Here is a statement from Dr. Cauthen."
Sydney handed the clipping to Everley and she
read her area secretary's words.

Many things about the
death of Bill Wallace
make us think of the
death of the Christ. The
authorities were envious
of his place in the
hearts of people. They
used falsehood to bring
charges against him. They
tried to represent him as
an agent of the American
Government, as the Jews
tried to represent Jesus
as one stirring up revolt
against Rome. They
sought to stir up public
sentiment by calling
large groups of people
together. They subjected
him to a bitter and cruel
imprisonment. Early in
his imprisonment it was
reported he was required
to empty toilet buckets
and do other such tasks.

Just as in the case of
Jesus the enemies of the
truth sought to discredit
his testimony by
declaring the disciples
had come and stolen away
his body. In Wuzhou the
Communists stated that
Dr. Wallace had died by
strangling himself. This
nobody believes even a
moment. It is obviously
an effort on the part
of Communists both to
discredit his testimony
and to leave themselves
free from the charge of
having taken his life.
. . .

In the death of Bill
Wallace, Communism
reveals its real
character as a movement
undertaking to destroy
that which Christ stands
for. As it exerts its
energy against the people
of Christ, however, it
will be repeatedly made
evident that Christ's
people are willing to do
for the Lord today as
they have been throughout
the ages.

When she finished, Sydney, holding another article, said, "A doctor voiced my own feelings, though. This came from the journal of the International College of Surgeons."

He read the clipping:

```
Such men as this are the
soul of the college. In
their humility no less
than in their strengths
lies the embodiment of
the ideals that beckon
us all .... The Chinese
Communist Party, in its
valiant efforts to remake
the world, found Bill
Wallace's presence in
China an inconvenience.
He was a living example
of all they abhorred.
More than that, he had
an influence, quiet as he
was. No selfless life is
devoid of effects upon
others.
```

Sydney took his glasses off and looked at his wife, then at the nurse who had served alongside his brother-in-law. "From what we are constantly hearing, we know that William's life is going to continue to mean much to the kingdom of God. I believe he is going to mean even more in ways we will never hear about. I refuse to count his life a tragedy. It was a beautiful life, lived with a magnificent purpose that was and is being realized."

Everley's eyes were moist. "I keep remembering the Scripture verse they put on his grave, 'For to me to live is Christ.' The rest of the Scripture passage says, 'and to die is gain.'"

Afterword

Sydney Stegall believed Bill's life would influence others long after his death. He was right. In 1985, Bill's remains were brought from his burial place in Wuzhou to Knoxville, Tennessee, the place of his birth. He was buried in a cemetery not far from where he grew up.

Dr. Jim McCluskey brought a message at Bill's memorial service. At the time, Dr. McCluskey was the pastor of Wallace Memorial Baptist Church. The church started in the early 1950s and was named in memory of Bill Wallace. At the memorial service in 1985, Dr. McCluskey said, "The remains of Dr. William Lindsey Wallace cannot be contained in a box, in a grave, in Knoxville, Tennessee. What remains of William Lindsey Wallace is eternal in its essence and its influence."

From its beginning until now, Wallace Memorial Baptist Church has promoted missions. The church is committed to sharing the gospel with those who have never heard in Knoxville and around the world. The church has trained countless men and women who are now serving as Christian workers around the world.

I am grateful to be a part of the Wallace Memorial family. My life was personally influenced by Bill's life and legacy. I first read Jesse Fletcher's book, *"Bill Wallace of China,"* on which this book is based, when I was twelve or thirteen years old. Inspired by Dr. Wallace's example, I later accepted God's call to full-time Christian service. Later, in my twenties, my husband and I joined Wallace Memorial Baptist Church. The church fueled our love for missions and provided a vision and the training that motivated us to move forward in our calling to international missions.

In 1999 my family and I moved to Manila, Philippines, and for fifteen years we served overseas in East and Southeast Asia as missionaries with the International Mission Board, the same organization that sent Dr. Wallace to China all those years ago. Although I never visited Wuzhou, I visited Wallace Memorial Baptist Hospital in Pusan, South Korea. The hospital was started by missionary Rex Ray, and nurse Lucy Wright served there. When we lived in Seoul, the South Korean staff of the hospital routinely made trips into difficult areas in South Asia to provide medical care and to share the gospel with an unreached people group. They were continuing the legacy of Dr. Wallace.

What about you? God continues to call people who are willing to serve him. He might be calling you to be a doctor like Dr. Wallace or a nurse like Everley Hayes and Lucy Wright. He might be calling you to be a teacher or an engineer or an administrator. Whatever work He leads you to, He wants you to use your skills and gifts to tell others about Him. It may be in the place where you live now or in a place you have never heard of.

All He wants is for you to be available. Are you willing to say "yes" to whatever God is calling you to do?

Ann Lovell
Richmond, Virginia
Jan. 2019

Acknowledgements

Many people are responsible for this version of the Bill Wallace story for middle grade readers. First of all, I'm grateful to the late Dr. Jesse Fletcher, who captured Dr. Wallace's life and ministry in his 1963 book, "*Bill Wallace of China.*" I first met Dr. Fletcher in 1996 at an IMB appointment service at Wallace Memorial Baptist Church. Later in 2015, I talked with him again in Richmond, Virginia, as we celebrated the 50th anniversary of IMB's journeyman program, which he started.

In 2017 after speaking about Dr. Wallace's legacy at Wallace Memorial, I contacted Dr. Fletcher and asked his permission to use his book as the basis of a book geared toward 10- to 12-year-olds on the life of Bill Wallace. Dr. Fletcher graciously gave me his permission. Sadly, Dr. Fletcher died June 14, 2018, at age 87. He lived a long and distinguished life of service. For this version of the story and for his inspiration as a writer with a heart for missions and missionary stories, I owe him a debt of gratitude.

I'm also indebted to Dr. Fletcher's son, Scott, who gave his support to the project and shares the vision of making the Bill Wallace story come alive to a new generation of kids.

When I asked Dr. Jim McCluskey, pastor emeritus of Wallace Memorial, what he thought about a kids' book on Bill Wallace, he gave me his whole-hearted support. Throughout the process of putting this book together, Jim has been a source of encouragement and wisdom. I am grateful.

Cheryl Lewis, a former children's editor at LifeWay and a very good friend, provided outstanding editorial support. This book is stronger because of her knowledge and expertise.

Mike Mirabella, a children's illustrator, provided the cover art. Mike and I have worked together on a number of children's projects through the years. I am grateful he chose to lend his talents to this project as well.

Scott Peterson, who works in global research with the IMB, provided the historical photos and copies of Dr. Fletcher's journals without hesitation when I asked for them. I appreciate the efforts of the IMB to secure and safeguard missionary stories for this and future generations.

Most of all, I'm thankful to my husband, Joe, and my daughters, Lauren and Alli, who provide unwavering support for each new idea and project I undertake. Without them, life would be colorless.

Ann Lovell

Made in the USA
Middletown, DE
16 February 2019